THE BUTTERFLY CONVENTION

Susan Nadler

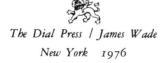

The Dial Press / James Wade

New York 1976

for Jack, for Jake, for Jackson

The 1976 publication of my book, The Butterfly Convention, caused an incendiary rift between my father and me. I don't think he ever got over my imprisonment or my drug smuggling ways.

In the 1985 release of Good Girls Gone Bad , a collection of stories about middle class women in white collar crime, I included a chapter about my own experience in prison.* I told the story of the love affair between myself and the head of the Baja Federalis that took place in that primitive yet strangely romantic hospital cell where I lived for five months .I had never told the story before out of fear of my father's anger.

My father never acknowledged the affair, even after my countless appearances on national television to promote Good Girls Gone Bad. It remained the unspoken truth between us. I was an outlaw and self anointed rebel – a product of the outrageous 60's and psychedelic 70's.

Susan Nadler

Nashville, TN

*This chapter is following the Butterfly Convention starting on page 185.

THE BUTTERFLY CONVENTION

1

*H*eat has a tendency to slow me down—which is something I greatly need. Actually, I like being slower better, because I do things more thoroughly—and my hands don't shake. It was about 104 degrees outside, and lethargy was a goal. Sleep was something you had to fight off, knowing you'd never be able to sleep at night. My father was in the left part of the garden—with the gardener. It made such an incongruous picture: this old, brown, wrinkled, slow-stepping, Mexican earth-lover, dressed in browns and grays—and my Brooks Brothers-pink-shirted, business executive, nimble-mover father. The gardener spoke no English, but needed help to operate the new Americano sprinkler. He had no bottom front teeth and kept his blue bandanna tied around his neck. My father spoke no Spanish and gently helped give the earth its water—through modern machinery.

Three butterflies came toward the slats in the window. I prayed they wouldn't mistakenly venture in through the plastic spaces into the hallway. It was oppressively hot there, and there was no exit for them. But they glided in and began the long search for the way out. Many times I tried to rescue these friends by calmly walking up and slowly, slowly approaching them with cupped hands; to gather them in—so as not to touch their fragile wings—and try to make them unafraid—so that they wouldn't hurt themselves in my "net." But generally my hands shook too much. My energies were too nervous and I would end up chasing them all over the hospital hallway—

with my oh-so-sleepy guards thinking that I was trying to make my long-promised, so widely publicized escape. I didn't feel like going through that routine again. But the heat had slowed me down—and my hands didn't shake. I had no shoes on and my feet made no noise on the bare floor; I cupped my hands together and slowly, patiently, and without nervousness approached the two blue-and-green larger ones, who looked like they had come to rest on the window crank. I asked for a little peace and quiet and lowered my hands until both butterflies pulled their two wings together like one—and trustingly fluttered onto my sweaty palms. With my eyes never leaving their wings, I slipped my hands through the window slats and the butterflies flew over toward the gardener, my father, and the water. Why couldn't someone lift me up into his hands and slip me out into the air? I would take wing and sing—oh, so happy to be free again. Why couldn't I free myself, my essence, from my body, my physical condition, and step outside my body, leave the shell behind, fly outside my mind into time without end. But no hands came, and the guard, my lonely friend Francisco, called me back to play gin with him, the sky got gray, perpetually threatening rain, and the electricity went off again. My father and the gardener turned off the sprinkler and somehow, with hands pointed toward the sky, communicated to each other that there would be no need for water—because "Maybe, *señor*—there would be some rain." To people who never see it, and live in hot lands, rain is very precious.

The heat reminded me of the *khamseen,* or sandstorms, that periodically hit Jerusalem in the summer months. There, I would close the windows during the day, lie on the cold, stone floor and drink water out of an Arab clay vessel. Then at dusk, during the hazy hours when the sunset was fighting for air, we would open the windows, let the stale air out, take cold showers, and smoke mentholated hashish joints to keep it together for the evening. All desert climates are the same; Baja and Israel and the Arab and Mexican mentalities are very similar—and equally slow. Another hot day, another hot memory.

The backs of my knees were sweating now and I lifted my sticky hospital gown, or *bata,* a little higher, sat on the edge of the bed— and waited for my father to come in, so dejectedly, to play our game with Francisco. Mexican gin is different from any other kind. You each get ten cards, and cannot pick up a card and put it into your hand unless you lay down two with it; in other words, all the cards must be used to make a triplicate. It is infinitely more difficult to play. Francisco, like all the guards or *policía* who worked the hospital detention cell, loved to play cards with me and my father; it helped pass the boring afternoons. It also kept them from dozing off and twitching nervously in their sleep. They would awaken jerkily at the first sound—thinking it was their *capitán,* or the *comandante* of the jail, or the district prosecutor, who would call them incompetent and threaten to fire them. But it never happened, because I always kept watch in the hallway for them. When they would doze off, I would daydream or read or study Spanish or cry. Isolation leads to the keen development of the senses. Any footstep could be categorized, for the hallway was long and the echoes loud. The Hospital Salvitorre, flat and on one level, where I stayed, was one of the few respectable hospitals in Mexico with a detention cell on the premises. It was a very strange setup, especially to spend three months in. My cell was designed for isolation and prevention of escape. Built into a separate and detached wing once occupied by prisoners and T.B. patients, now abandoned by all except prisoners, it was directly in line with the kitchen—where the doors remained open and all the heat would slowly drift down the thirty-foot corridor. The hallway that led to my cell was about two and one-half feet wide and was windowed all the way with heavy glass and Venetian slats. My cell was at the end of the corridor. It was set up with heavy bars instead of a door—and a huge lock. There was a three by five foot square directly in front of the cell on which stood a small table with a barred window above it. The guards sat here during their twelve-hour watches. The cell itself was about ten by fifteen feet, about the same size as my cell at the Edificio M. Sobarzo—the local jail where I spent my first month. The cell walls were white. My room had two beds, a bathroom without windows, and a little porch. Ironically, the patient-prisoner who had lived there before me had broken the glass separating the room from the porch, so there was no protection from rain or heat. The porch had walls of cement ten feet thick, and where the roof should have been were heavy bars—again to prevent escape. I would sit on the cement outside at night hoping for a breeze to shoot down through the bars, trying to distinguish the stars from the reflections of the metal. By listening to the footsteps I could tell if a nurse or an orderly, the *comandante,* or my father approached.

Daytime, the porch was extraordinarily hot, and since there was no other furniture, I would sit on the lumpy bed and try to differentiate the footsteps from the other hospital noises. These footsteps were slow and yet springy-masculine, not plodding like the weary police. Happy, like the dedicated interns, yet somehow sorrowful— my father.

The small fan made nothing cooler. He stood for a moment in front of it, wiping his forehead off with his immaculately white handkerchief. He smiled at fat little Francisco, my guard and our friend, drank some of my warm grapefruit juice, looked around, pulled his chair up to the bed, and chuckled as Francisco hustled to bring his chair in for our gin game. Thank God, they now trusted me enough to leave the cell unlocked; somehow it made me feel a little freer. Francisco's police uniform was beige, his skin brownish. My father's hand was chalky white. My hands started to shake again. Life for me is a series of crashes with reality.

"Susanita, mucho calor, tu padre está no bien feliz." (Susan, it's very hot and your father looks very unhappy.)

Thanks Francisco, I know how unhappy my father is.

"What did he say?"

"He said you looked very hot and he hoped you were ready to play."

"Oh sure, damn hot. You feel all right Susan? You look a little pale."

"Sure Daddy, much better."

Why do my hands shake so much with him? My stomach is knotty and I feel like shit. And I had a sharp memory of my gentle father two days earlier bringing my breakfast of a soft roll and jelly

6

from the hotel in the city where he was to stay for this trip down, his third to Baja. We had talked about life, and the state of the union. And how a former Wisconsin SDSer, namely, his daughter-me-I-liar-cheat-dope-pusher, feels about a President like Nixon; what makes his corruption more acceptable than mine. And for one minute the only man in my life I had never seen swear, or be cruel, looked at me and said:

"The only goddamn reason I'm here, Susan, and your Mother is sick and crying, is because you wanted a fast screw and a faster dollar. You're a whorer of life, Susan. You pretend to find life so simple, wanting to smuggle hashish and retire to the country with a nonproductive bum like Andrew. Where were your goddamn values? And who do you think you are?" And then the tears, mine and his and then . . . "I'm your daughter and I'm sorry."

Why did I have to get caught, I'm protected-divine-a child of God-and I'm Susan-who the hell are you-just my father-and then more tears. But thinking now, Daddy, is your getting me out of jail fair—considering the law, and my guilt? Is your attempting to get me out better than my smuggling? And yet I knew that without him to get me out, I would be there for many years.

"Susana—está a tú." (It's your turn.)

I threw down my third Jack and Francisco chuckled because he knew I thought I would win again. Juanita, the dark, thin, heavily mustached nurses' aide, brought us back a pitcher of iced lemonade—she had a crush on my father. Francisco hid his cards in the sheets, pretending to be just talking to us. He couldn't get caught playing cards; perhaps someone would report it to the *comandante.* Actually, no one really cared. I jumped out of bed, happy for the interruption and relief from my hideous memories, grabbed Juanita and tickled her until she cried and I teasingly called her *flacita,* or the skinny one. She ran down the hall. Francisco laughed—he thought I was a star. My father shook his head as if thinking, "She still doesn't know the seriousness of life or her crime—or her sentence." And I thought, "If I can just keep laughing. Life may be a carnival, but jail—either real or emotional—and especially in a foreign country—it's a motherfucker."

*R*ightfully, this chapter should be entitled "The Lower-Level Boogie," because my boogie got lower and I hit new depths of self-deception as I entered into the Baja caper. It could be called, "How did a nice Jewish princess like you, from such a culturally oriented, educated, well-rounded (I'll say) background end up in a Mexican jail?" Or, "Why did I want or need to smuggle 500 kilos of hash, or did I know what I was doing?" Or I could call it "Fucking On the Fairy Side, or How a Fast Fuck and a Fast Dollar Ran My Life." But self-degradation definitely is not constructive nor does it help one to become closer to one's self. Because knowing isn't enough—once you know, you have to do something about it. I always kind of floated through life—like an opium dreamer. I left my radical SDS and Kill for Peace University of Wisconsin days, and floated to Israel—Ashdod, for an archeological dig. I liked the freer vibes there, and was lucky enough to get a full scholarship to the University of Jerusalem. There I met my photographer-cameraman-artist-student-Israeli husband. So far, all had fitted in with my mother's and father's planning and grooming lessons.

However, my wacked-out LSD nights-on-the-floor visions were not completely consistent with their wishes. So I tactfully omitted to tell them that I was discontented for reasons beyond my control and desperately looking for my spirit—which was nowhere to be found. Living in a foreign country had great merits for me. My husband and I took *tiuls,* or excursions, every weekend, and saw where Sampson met Delilah and where King David was buried. We ran from the bombs and sympathized with young Israel. I watched as my radical young husband became more sympathetic to the Palestinian guerrillas as our Arab friends in the Old City of Jerusalem paid higher and higher taxes. I became seriously interested in Cabala, or Jewish mysticism, and coming closer to God—and as I came closer to God, I got further and further away from my husband, who was more interested in painting cemeteries and distorted figures groping in hell. We smoked a lot of hashish—moved to the Armenian section of the Old City and bought opium from the laundryman called Jacob's father. The Old City smelled of camels and *pita* (Arab bread) and spices and exotic cloth and tension. Our Alexandria Quartet species of existence became harder—more defined. We traveled to London, Paris, Dublin, and Cyprus looking for peace of mind—which we neither minded nor peacefully approached. We had to maintain this image of "classy freaks" and believe me, I felt like a D-movie heroine. The harder we tried to be in the trip, the worse it got, with acid confrontations and an occasional beating for me. My husband used to tell me to go away for a while and not bother him.

Then one day I found a seventeen-year-old Californian who talked to me of freedom—and health food and sunshine and music (à la West Coast) and making love, not war, and tenderness; and all the inexperience of youth and mescaline mellowness of the West Coast— which is vacuous and good-vibrationed out with Jesus freaks, Krishna freaks, drug freaks, health freaks, and fuck freaks, but mellow man, very mellow. And my husband, who was always too busy being productive to talk to me, as I stood in his shadow and wondered what the hell I was doing here in this creation, would say to me (long before Women's Lib had its day) "go talk to Ivan and his mystical Rabbi friends," Ivan being the seventeen-year-old. Oh Israel, why do you have such heavy karma that your youth are hard from fighting so long and protecting their little piece of land and family, and your children don't even know any fairy tales? And so I talked to Ivan and his friend Rabbi Itzak, the twenty-three-year-old mystic who turned me on to Cabala. We talked and talked until we saw it rain from the same cloud and I got divorced from my husband. And Ivan and I went to live on a mountain top high in Jerusalem—and instead of studying spiritualism, we read Marvel comic books and marveled at love and methedrine, and my psychedelic haze occupied all my thoughts. Life is so simple when your parents support you. We wanted to continue our dream in L.A. and decided to smuggle some hash in along with us. So we got an Israeli police official to send it out for us to Los Angeles—in religious books. We laughed at the simplicity of money. When we got busted, Ivan's religious, orthodox mother called in a rabbi for help. And because a helpful California official was Jewish and wanted to help out Jewish youth, we were never formally arrested, just scared. However, we were never sure if we had a record with Interpol or even the L.A.P.D. But apparently we were not scared enough. We couldn't make it in the reality of working, and we broke up, penniless, without our mountain top.

After that, life had very little time for me. Alone and in L.A., I continued my search for the Holy Grail. I found SDS replaced by more violent Weathermen after my two years' absence. Uncle Tim Leary never told me that turning on was easy, dropping out only requires a little guts, but trying to tune in, that's the trick.

I went from hashish to seconals and finally hit cocaine—the rich kids' drug. I discovered rock stars in Rolls-Royces collecting unemployment, and all the beautiful people who worked so hard to be mellow and beautiful that had never even heard of Dylan. And to be really hip—I mean to make the scene—was to live next door to Yvette Mimieux in a four-bedroom house with a pool in Benedict Canyon, wear old denim, and drive either a funky pickup truck or an old Rolls. And when you pulled out a diamond coke spoon everyone knew, oh man, she's one of those enlightened ones—let's all go out and eat salads in the smog on Sunset Strip and buy $150 shirts to wear with our faded dungarees so everyone knows that we're not materialistic. Get high with Dallas Taylor and Stephen Stills—

remember them, the Topanga Canyon boys who wrote about the new reality and the country? Then let's go home, shoot heroin and O.D. And still, everyone talked about moving to the country and getting on with the simple life. And whole wheat bread and being high on life and hey brother and sister—and that's all they did, they talked. The talkers, not the doers, and I was one of them. No peace of mind, a lot of vitamins, a lot of mystical, astrological, numerological, Brotherhood of the Light, cosmological, full on in the divine, jive-ass talk. And no one worked or had even a piece of clay to be proud of. Then everyone went electric, eclectic, and hard rock.

Sometimes I would stop—in my travels from bed to bed or from city to city—and say, "Wait a minute, what the hell, how did I get from twenty-one on a dig in Ashdod, ban the bomb, and at least read a book—to twenty-five, still a lot of jive-soaper madness?" I then went from L.A. to Mill Valley, where everyone is an unemployed Ph.D. turned carpenter or plumber with $50,000 in the bank—yeah, here we are, self-realized Jewish middle class, definitely not in the trip, paying $500 a month rent and thinking we live close to the land. But it's the same all over.

In Colorado, everyone has blond hair and believes in clean air, a lot of turquoise, and clean cocaine—oh yeah, skiing. Finally on the beach, living by myself, twenty miles north of Acapulco, in Pie de la Cuesta, where the sunsets are truly sea-shattering and the waves are famous for their height and body-bending capacity. Sometimes, at night, I would sit on the beach and watch when Venus was so close to the moon—I thought that they kissed—and say, "If only I had enough money, I would buy land and not have to work and get straight and find God"—the quest of my generation. But I never thought in terms of "Why not start now?" Because when you fool yourself enough into talking about spiritualism, you start to have delusions of grandeur. You know, a little knowledge about Egypt, a few joints of Acapulco gold, a few male reinforcements and you just know you're Cleopatra, this lifetime. You're divine. And when the Messiah comes, you'll walk in a white robe by his side and he'll shine his ever-loving light on you, because you're a star. Then I would amble back to the old hotel where I was staying and swing on a hammock, drink a little tequila or marijuana milkshake, shoot a little codeine, for the pain of being a lonely woman, so pretty and so alone, and go to sleep for the night, reinforced by my friends, who were the same wherever I went. They were unemployed, maybe from wealthy families, and hated democracy and capitalism because America never realized their worth. I sold my old ruby ring for $100 so that I could stay for the next month on that money. Then I took my blanket and headed for the beach to figure out the tides, how much a kilo of dope would cost, and to correlate my own system for numerology and astrology.

At this point you may say, here's another product of the stupendous sixties, and what is she leading up to? This is all just background to show how I ended up on March 10, 1972, on the beach in Mexico, getting an airmail telegram from my lawyers in L.A. to the effect that my long-forgotten automobile accident of two years ago had paid off. Please fly back immediately and collect $15,000. Do not pass go. . . . My dream had come true.

I returned to L.A. and collected my $15,000 at the bank. I went through all the red tape, thanked my lawyers, who got one third of the settlement, and my doctors, who got one third of the settlement, and retired to Hollywood to think about what I would do with my $5,000 share. I had several options, for the first time in many years. I could take the money and go to Mendocino, get a small place and live there, or go back to Acapulco nights of golden moondances, or try to somehow double the small amount. As it would happen, like Harry Karma would say, I ran into an old friend of mine, a blond, long-haired, definitely "hey sister," full on in the divine, upper-Hollywood lover, Gemini song writer, ex-Laurel Canyon redwood lover. So he says to me, says Andrew, "Hey sister, let's have us a feast to celebrate St. Patrick's Day." And we went to Quinn's health food store on Melrose Boulevard, and bought us a lot of organic goodies. Andrew called up all the brothers, with his ol' lady glaring at me, reassured by his "she's an old friend" routine, and suddenly twenty assorted Hollywood ex-hippy love children were gathered in Andrew's split-level, balconied, stained-glass-windowed apartment on North Sweetzer. There were mandalas and pillows and Moroccan tapestries and sandalwood incense and Moroccan *kif* to get our heads together. And Andrew and I in the kitchen making, of all St. Patrick's Day food, potato pancakes and Caesar salad.

In Los Angeles, as in practically no other city I've been, relationships start very casually. This is because, as everyone sits around in caftans and drinks wine, the vibes are sort of loose, so to speak. The slightest eyebrow raise or candid smile smacks of invitation, because you are free, sisters and brothers under the sun, and, incidentally, under the robes. The slightest sign, such as a rainbow reflection in the toaster behind your heads, and you know that you two are meant to be. Andrew's and my sign came in a more mundane, but definitely kinetic-energy or parapsychological way. The kitchen was pretty smoky from all the dope and pancakes and I asked him, "Honey" (endearing term of old friends), "please open the window," which mysteriously dropped open of its own accord, and obviously meant that the powers above had destined us for each other. So, many pancakes later, and sixteen friends' departure closer to the real nitty gritty of the night, Andrew asked his girl friend to sleep downstairs and we climbed, rather clumsily, up the wooden stairway to one of the most beautiful, fabulous bedrooms ever. It was very clean and California-styled glass and wood, with high beams that faced the west, where the sun set. A small latticed window looked out on the trees, the moon, and the stars. The bed was very simply made of wood and about three feet tall; foam rubber cushions replaced the mattress and the top was covered with about $2,000 worth of furs. The room was very small, with built-in closets. The east windows were next to a simple wooden shelf that held books like *Somewhere Over Rainbow Bridge* and *Mastery,* and all kinds of jars of jewels and colored glass incense holders and a tie-dyed satin shawl and boxes with old coins and stones. I was never terribly good at these first-time bedroom scenes, and proceeded in my Aries naïveté, my never-stop-to-consider-the-consequences manner, to tell old friend Andrew, who was now offering me cocaine on a spoon of the crescent moon and star, about my financial situation.

He was quiet and pensive for a while. Then we talked for the next seven hours about how I could invest my money in his deal, so perfectly set up (aren't they all?), and stay in the apartment with him and maybe fly to Mexico, only this time Baja, and get back ten times my investment, which made my $4,000 investment quickly turn into a $40,000 caper. Then we reassured each other how both of us ". . . snort, pass that joint, baby . . ." were interested in writing music and being close to the earth, living simply (". . . where did you get those divine furs?"), and taking care of all of our ". : . high friends." We would do this by buying land in the north of California and building houses for our big Karmic family, and wearing robes and making music, and definitely not getting high (". . . do you have a roach clip?"). This was it, man, we had found each other, both vegetarians and readers of Gurdjieff, liked Van Morrison and Jackson Brown, and had a common goal. Now all we had to do was fall in love and work out the finances. Another fuck on the fairy side.

Morning, morning—it seems so peaceful in the morning, and I drowsily awoke to Andrew's arms around me and fur in my mouth. We talked. Conspirators, whose ends naturally justified the means or vice versa. There was no way either of us could ever get caught. The plan was that I would leave for San Francisco to stay in Fairfax with friends for three days. Andrew would get rid of his ol' lady, contact the deal people, and set up the transaction.

I left that afternoon, exhilarated, and landed in San Francisco to be met by the two people who perhaps best lived and believed in the life style we all talked about. Fairfax is a lovely residential area not too far from San Francisco, calm and peaceful. My friends spoke of freedom without drugs, they talked of real brotherhood, without drug-induced states, they walked naturally, ate well, and warned me not to invest money in drugs. "Settle down Susan, get to the point of living. . . ." I got the hell out of there.

Three days later I flew back and moved in with Brother Andrew who had kindly offered to temporarily house old friends—two Sufi homosexuals, who were mystics, composers, and export-import specialists. Things were so flowsy at this home that I soon forgot to really question my plan with Andrew and just accepted my position as cook, cleaner, lover, heavy-duty woman, and seer-mystic. After all, flattery can get you anywhere.

How I gave away my $5,000 is interesting. I had $4,000 of it in twenties in an envelope in the closet. Andrew and I decided to keep $1,000 of mine and $1,000 of his (or maybe only my) money, for living expenses. He would wait until the Big Man (Ted) had left for Morocco to ship out the hash. They sent it out in a foolproof manner. I mean they were big-time, Andrew and his buddies; they had apartments in La Paz, Morocco, L.A., Vegas, and Nepal. Ted would call Andrew to leave for Mexico and he would go down there to receive the package. Meanwhile, back at the ranch, I would stay in L.A. for two or three weeks, keep Andrew's car, buy some expensive clothes, keep the two Sufi brothers happy, and carry on the Word for the both of us until Andrew wired for me to come down. It was so logical. There were three partners, one of whom was Andrew, the lowest, because he had the least amount of money to invest. The three of them had a phony land-development company, with an office, business cards and even a young, slightly shady lawyer, who certainly came into play later. They worked hard to maintain their fronts as respectable gents—nice clothes, Gucci, Pucci, and suede. They worked hardest at living two lives. Hip and wealthy, straight on the outside, freaky and get-down-to-it on the inside. They endured more hours of irritation than the average nine-to-fiver. Anyhow, one morning in late March, Ted appears at 7:30, dressed in a three-piece suit, with a smashing bag, limousine waiting—ready to go to Morocco. My first encounter with the man, and he refuses to discuss business with me—after all, who am I except for the funder of this deal, or the sucker. He takes my envelope and slithers out for his plane. Andrew hears Ted promise to wire him in two weeks when the package is ready, to leave for Mexico, Baja, and pick it up. We go back to sleep after he leaves, me $4,000 and a lot of security shorter.

The next week was very luxurious, and fun. The two awakened spiritualists, Andrew and I, who don't care about money and want a simple place in the country, run all over town, buying $100 sun glasses, eating $50 meals, snorting coke, and staying in bed until two in the afternoon. We visit dealer friends high in Bel Air, whose butlers show us into Tudor rooms where we artfully snort the big H, with an occasional movie director and his old lady, a has-been or would-be actress. At night—or in the wee hours of the morning—we read yoga books and go to Canter's for bagels, along with the 5:00 A.M. winos and the left-over partyers. We finally get the telegram and Andrew tearfully leaves for Mexico—"Honey, you'll be with me soon."

I spend my waiting time taking speed from my respectable Beverly Hills doctor so I can fit into my bikini. I go to the dentist, buy clothes to fit the part of a hip business executive from the West Coast's ol' lady. I also help out the Sufi brothers by selling their Berber Moroccan jewelry to Jill St. John for her boutique in Aspen. I get lonely, but some of the brothers come over every night to make sure I'm all right. I get very high, do a lot of laundry, play the recorder and dream idyllic dreams of "our" land in the north. I also spend a lot of time thinking what a great job Andrew and I are doing for humanity. I get lonelier as time goes on and try to call Andrew, but he is in Baja in a sleepy little town called La Paz and they have only one telephone line going into it—every three days the rain washes it out and the wind blows it away.

Two weeks finally go by, and Andrew calls. He tells me to get on a plane the next morning; there's a ticket waiting for me at the airport. I'm to bring some money, a little dugie (heroin), and some coke. So, for the second time that year I'm going to board a plane for Mexico, although for a different part of the country, and live on the beach, although in a different life style. I had never even bothered to learn Spanish, because I was always so stoned, and related mainly to Americans. Secrecy was important, but it's hard to hide being a dealer on the international level. I said that Andrew was in

Canada and that I was going to meet him. On the plane I wore a large silver-and-turquoise cross that Andrew had made, carried my tan leather case, checked to see if all the dope was in my make-up case, took two quaaludes, and fell asleep as the Air Mexico plane left L.A. I was never to return there again.

*T*he minute I stepped off the plane—or rather, groggily shuffled off—I felt a tremendous wave of heat. I started sweating between my breasts—I felt it trickle down the pink halter top and hit the zipper on my pants—which were really Andrew's white jeans. Thanks to the lovely doctor in Beverly Hills—he looked after all the brothers and sisters in our family—and my fifty mg. obetrol speedsters, I was thin enough to fit into Andrew's size 29 jeans. I spotted him immediately as I glided off the plane stairs and tried to hold on to my already sweaty leather bag, wipe the droplets off my stomach, and see the boy through the glare. Tall Andrew, thin, blond sort of Richard Chamberlain, looking vague, held his straw (ethnic man, very ethnic) hat in his tanned hand and with his other arm, crushed me in a sweaty embrace.

"Hey honey, *señorita, qué pasa* with my baby?"

I kept looking at my sandals to avoid the discomfort I felt in his arms. He seemed so frail and the time of separation had clouded his image in my mind. But he was quick, as usual, to pick up on my vibes, and silently took my bag, admired the old Moroccan coin around my neck (courtesy of the Sufi brothers), and guided me to the Safari jeep the company rented. He talked effortlessly and slowly, like one of the Mexicans. The La Paz airport was very clean, the people looked Mexican, and yet I felt that it was different here from on the mainland. However, one value was unchanged. Every male eye in the vicinity focused in on my semi-exposed, bra-less breasts. Yet these brown eyes were not licentious, like the Arabs or the Mexican gigolos in Acapulco—these were rather dreamy, and respectful of womanhood.

"Honey, did you bring the coke and dope?" I, of course, would never have forgotten this. And Andrew told me, as he smoked his Winston to the filter, how easy our life down here would be, and how much he had missed me, about our apartment and his friends, the beach and the restaurants. It was a very wealthy and laid-back life. As we drove to my new home, my eyes searched the immaculate and steaming streets of La Paz for a beggar with outstretched hand, of the sort that decorated so many of the streets in Mexico. I saw none that day, nor any in the five months I stayed in Baja. Maybe it is because La Paz is so close to California and the people are Americanized, or because these undiscovered men had great dignity, but no one ever begged or even tried to get a penny from the tourists. We continued our drive to our apartment on the beach road, and I saw the beautiful white sand and clear sea of Coromel, the beach I would spend so many days at with Andrew and think of so longingly when I was in jail. The town itself was very quiet. La Paz is a duty-free port, Andrew explained to me, and consequently much of its money comes from importing low and making marginal profit on perfume, sweaters, Oaxaca straw bags, Taxco silver, and mainland embroidered shirts. Because it was so sleepy—and an open port—Andrew and Ted chose it to ship the hash into. Large packages aroused very little suspicion there.

The tourist who frequents La Paz is entirely different from the tourist in Mexico City or Acapulco. They are primarily Waspy yachting types. There were many yachts moored there, and a whole subculture of the inbred fishermen scooted from boat to boat in little motor craft—very snobbish, Bing Crosby types. They frequented the town only to buy Kahlua and drink coffee at La Perla, the major sidewalk café. The town had no university, so most of the young people either left for Guadalajara University or stayed at home to become busboys at one of the four hotels, waiters at restaurants, fishermen, or police. Life was very simple in La Paz. Baja is one of the very few unexplored territories left in the Northern Hemisphere.

This was all fine with me. The people were generally more friendly—less out to hustle the Americans. In sophisticated places, all the natives had a con or come-on. I detested that, it made me feel like a piece of meat or a roll of bills, that's all.

Even La Paz is becoming prey to modern man and advanced technology. The government had decided to build a road from Tijuana to La Paz to expedite travel and open up tourism. It also planned to refurbish the phone lines. As the road got closer to completion, more and more prostitutes appeared looking for work and gringo money, more young Mexican drifters and dopesters happened onto the scene. But my first impression never left me. The older sections of town, with the roosters that crowed to the tune of Ac-a-pul-cooooo, and the mud houses of reds and browns looked like Desolation Road from Dylan's song. We came through the city proper, which was small and slightly sophisticated with its banks, little specialty stores, and many *farmacias.* Finally we passed the docks and one modern building—Hospital Salvitorre, across the street from our apartment.

La Paz, or, literally translated, "Peace," was calm and had a quiet aura, as I imagined some old Western towns of Utah and Wyoming once were. Andrew had done a good job with his little tour-guiding, and the joint we had smoked on the way had calmed me down. He had introduced me to a town that he had known I would love. Finally he told me that the crime rate was very low—the trouble mostly arose from the *borrachos*—or drunks—petty theft and wife-beating. Occasionally a prostitute would be hauled in for carrying diseases. The police were the highest paid of the lowly civil jobs—respected, and yet impotent—they were not permitted to carry guns. The citizens were afraid of a drunken policeman with a weapon. No American had ever been busted for drugs in this sleepy city, and the police were really not that concerned with drug users. My new home consisted of a few class B-plus restaurants for the tourists Andrew had pointed out to me, a few *orchata,* or rice-water stands, a central commercial, or supermarket, many fresh-fruit stands and tortilla stands, and much serenity and peace. We started walking toward the stairs to our apartment, which was in a complex

of about fifteen, owned by a Mr. Cortezar and his two junkie sons—
Pablo and José. They were both good friends of Andrew's, instinc-
tively understood his business, and kept to themselves. Mr. Cortezar
tried his hardest to be respectable, but had little luck, despite his
wealth, for everyone knew his sons were "into drugs." The apartment was modern, had two bedrooms, a bathroom, kitchen, and
dining and living room combined; it smelled clean and like the sea.
The decorations were from Morocco and India, left over from other
dope shipments. Mandalas covered the walls, a little plastic sculpture of Krishna and his pals playing various instruments sat on the
dining room table and the doorways held chimes and mobiles from
Tangiers and maps of Mexico. We were a wealthy couple in land development, who went out to eat frequently, swam, stayed on an occasional yacht, and kept to ourselves. I wondered how long we could
keep up that image when we got loaded and didn't care. Not too
long as I was to see. Andrew broke my reverie by announcing that
most of the dope came from Mazatlán, and was good—not outstanding. The *farmacias* had all the mandrax (French equivalent of quaaludes) that we could eat, and with my good looks, who knew what
else we could score.

I was very happy. An all-expense-paid trip to the hotlands, a
beautiful apartment, a man who at least dug me, all the drugs we
wanted, and an assured $40,000 coming. What else could you
want, but a little brains, common sense, foresight and self-respect?
But when you take a lot of drugs you forget about self-respect. It
goes down your throat along with all the other respects you know,
because you really can't like yourself too much to take all the drugs
to forget yourself. So we undressed, put on our respective bikinis,
snorted some coke and headed for Coromel Beach. Once there, it
was like every other beach, hot, sandy, and waveless. We jumped
around, all coked up—swam, laughed, ate fish soup, and went
home. I gave Andrew his welcoming present, a $75 roach clip I had
had made for him out of amber, an old Mexican coin, and turquoise.
We showered, and José Cortezar, our neighbor and slightly incoherent friend, stopped over to meet Andrew's lady. We smoked some
pot and decided to go out for dinner, very spiffy, but we moved too

quickly to be considered really mellow. I dressed up in my two-inch clogs, halter top and tie-dyed pants, thinking I looked very straight. On the way to dinner we decided to stop at the first *farmacia.* After all, we looked respectable, didn't we? (We were so crazy.) I had worked a one-month stint at a hospital, as a venapuncture artist, in Pittsburgh, so I had a hospital identification card that had no expiration date on it. I'll tell you one thing, I thought as I walked into the *farmacia,* I never had missed a vein, I was a junky's delight. Ah, yes, *Señorita,* a nurse. I got two twenty-five pill bottles of mandrax, and a lot of wolf calls. I got into our jeep, popped two pills, Andrew popped two, and we started the next month of oblivion.

Sometimes at night, loaded on our asses, we would go to a steamy discotheque, drink Banana Daiquiris, and sensuously dance with a group of young Bajans clapping around us as if we were heroes. That was our trip—reckless, footloose and fancy free. We had a certain charisma that all conspirators have; we knew something that no one else did. We had begun to fall in love—rather expectedly for our story. It's very easy to fall in love with all expenses paid—in a tropical paradise—doped out of your mind. Soon we discovered that we both liked music. Andrew played his guitar like a third-class Dylan, wailing. I sang like a third-class Joni Mitchell, who wrote Judy Collins-type lyrics. We decided that we would take our money, buy land in Northern California, get recording equipment, and make records. Another drug delusion, the Sonny and Cher of the coke generation. We were great, so we heard from our friends José and Pablo, even though they didn't understand English too well. Where was I at, I ask myself now? Nothing daunted me, and Andrew made me feel that we were talented. I did not have my own values in these situations, my parents had always decided what was good for me to hear and now that I was a rebel I assumed that anything they wouldn't like was all right. They definitely wouldn't have liked this music. I rebelled against their values, I merely became "against," and whatever I wasn't against, I was for. So I let myself listen to Andrew about the music, about the drug deal. It took too much energy to think for myself. After all man, I'm too stoned to be bothered. But as we tried to write all night, the heat tired us out, the pills didn't help, so we would get up around ten or eleven in the morning, squeeze fresh orange juice, talk about the God in us—shining through if we could only open our eyes to see—drink *café con leche* at the Perla, read the local English-language newspaper and head for Coromel Beach—each of us wiped out by 11:30 A.M. on two mandrax.

All the people at the beach knew us; we were the two lovers who frequently stumbled into the water, nodded out a lot, and spent a lot of money on food and booze. Around three in the afternoon we'd head home, listen to our tape deck, take showers, make love, and pass out until seven or so when we'd wake up, usually with headaches, admire each other's tans, stay home, or go out to eat. Either way we'd smoke some dope, and if we stayed home we'd eat salads and chocolate pudding. This was our pattern. About nine or ten we'd start writing music—Andrew listening to my verses, and the two of us harmonizing and picking out the chords. We needed a pickup however, and our devious little minds let methedrine madness, the strung-out blues, enter our lives. We had shot speed before, and we figured that with our act, we could cop anything from the *farmacia*—especially the Day and Night Pharmacy which indeed stayed open all night. Before the month was out we had worn out our welcome at every local drug store—dried the town of mandrax, liquid valium, speed, and all the 26-point needles. We also had, most importantly, our own local pharmacist connection. We would pull up, I would go into the drugstore, flash my hospital card, get the needles and syringes first, and check out the speed department. The speed consisted mainly of pills that we would soak in water and pull up through cotton into our syringes—they were all very shootable—eskatrol, obetrol, desoxyn, ritalin—the list is endless. We would pay the small price—our lives—run home, and set up shop. Speed junkies are very organized and hygienic about details, because they are so spaced out that that's all they can handle, details, man. We used my beautiful Indian scarf to tie off our veins and would always go into our bathroom to get off. Normally Andrew would help me to get off first, because my veins were very shallow and I was too nervous to poke around. I reassured myself that anyone who couldn't get herself off was definitely amateurish, no chance I'd ever get addicted. Then I would get off and rush around like a mad dog, sterilize all the needles, and help my old man into the world of crazed dreams, delusions of grandeur, organization of nothing, and young-old, worn-out bodies. We would stay up all night—sweating, biting our lips, pounding out loud music, and recording it on the tape deck. One night I sang for seven hours straight—the same tune—my lips dry and cracked—hallucinating like crazy, my voice hoarse and going, going, gone. We would come down, or get tired, around six, and watch the incredible sunrise. It often looked like peach-colored faces smiling down on us. They were the winged children of the morning who helped us reorient ourselves and mellow out for a minute. Shortly thereafter we would get tired out and rush to the bathroom to get off again. That's the trouble with speed: you get so high you think you're being productive and sleep becomes the enemy that keeps you from your duties. So you shoot at night. In the morning, it starts to wear off more and more quickly, so you do it again and again until you finally pass out, exhausted, and sleep for twelve hours. In the morning, after getting off again and feeling renewed with energy, we would go down to the pier, fish, and sometimes fall into the water. Spaced out and worn thin all day, conversation between us was mainly short, personal, and communicable on the highest level—so we thought, however unintelligible it was to others. We got further and further away from the straight set we were trying to portray, and forgot why we were there. We were only coherent enough two or three times a week to remember the business deal. Dig it—we had been there for almost three weeks and only one word from Ted, in Morocco with the package. About three times a week, with much trouble trying to walk straight, and at great expense, we would go to one of the hotels and Andrew would place a person-to-person call to Aero Cargo, the small national airline that was supposed to fly the package in from Mexico City. Their headquarters were in San Diego, and Andrew always spoke to the same man, who told him that although they had notified Andrew that the package had been shipped from Morocco four weeks ago on a line that transferred it to

Aeronaves in Mexico proper, which then flew it straight to La Paz, without going through any risky American customs, so far no word had been received. We should have become suspicious then, but we were too confident in ourselves and our divine protection, and far too drugged out. We would write cryptic and symbolic letters to Ted, who was now back in L.A., and receive money from him, but no answers. Andrew assured me that Ted would contact us if anything was amiss, and continued our forty-dollar phone calls to San Diego. This time, approximately May 15, or around the time that George Wallace was shot, marked the beginning of our transition from Lower-Level Boogie to Loony Tunes. As we got stoned more intensely and more frequently, we were less and less able to keep it together and maintain an exterior of the straight couple. Everyone in town knew us—we never worked and spent a lot of money. One night, the night we totally blew it, we got some windowpane acid left over from the LSD rage of the mid-sixties. We had just dropped it and were preparing to watch the sunset, when José Cortezar, green-faced and zonked out, dropped in to tell us he had pure heroin from Mazatlán, and would we care to shoot it, which of course we would. We proceeded to alternately vomit, hallucinate, and laugh our way through town all night. Me in a long purple kaftan, sun glasses, and my huge turquoise cross, Andrew in his hat, jeans, T shirt, and beach towel converted to a cape. We cavorted through town all night, double-parking, knocking over all the glasses at the bars, vomiting and laughing, pulling up to the only restaurant open all night—Cielo Azul, The Blue Sky. We were so wrecked—our friendly old waiter came and served us in our car, but this was not park and eat in Hollywood, and we were not acting straight. After that evening, we both decided fuck it—fuck the image, which we had really only had in our minds, and we got really loose. Since we had exhausted the speed supply in La Paz, we would shoot any drug—I found myself more interested in the needle than the drug— ol' sex in a dropper. Liquid valium was all that we could find, so we shot liquid valium and nodded out at restaurants, fell over in the markets, and just generally got it on. Our paranoia about our image left us with the speed, as did our ability to perceive what was going on at all. It was May 22, Andrew had been there six weeks, me one month, there was no package, continuous bullshit from the airline, and the heat was becoming intense.

On May 23, I was sick from shooting so much methedrine and valium and I had my period again for the third time in a month. Andrew was weak, but still laughing. A knock on the door around one o'clock in the afternoon woke us and it was Ted, dressed to kill in a three-piece suit. He took one look at us, me hardly able to walk and Andrew a little shaky, and he knew the scene, thought maybe a night in the Guadalajara Hilton would help us. However, I was too sick and Andrew wouldn't go without me. Ted spent the hours before his plane reassuring us that all was well, turning us on to coke, which woke me right up, and being amazed at our situation. He left for Guadalajara to check out another deal and that evening Andrew and I received a telegram from Aero Cargo telling us that the package had arrived. I thought the telegram boy looked at us suspiciously, but we were both too lethargic or paranoid to act on my suspicion; we went out for a full-course meal and to call Ted at the Hilton.

However, I started to feel very nervous—perhaps Andrew told me I was nervous because I had been busted before, going back to L.A. Nevertheless, we went to sleep with visions of sugar plums and dollars dancing in our heads—and woke up to Ted at the door, jubilant and ready to pick up the package. Two hundred and fifty kilos of hashish. Another loony tune from yours truly. So far, so good . . .

*O*versatiated with dreams, she realized, Hey, man, they aren't what they seem. So she wakes up and it's another hot day in La Paz. She wonders—if this is life, what's the cause? And Susan says to Andrew, "It's our big day, the twenty-fourth of May, no time to play, what d'ya say? Let's get on our way." And Ted appears at the door, exactly like the day before, looking slightly bored. He says Guadalajara was very noisy and commercial. The closest I had ever gotten to Guadalarjara was the commercial on the radio where the operatic tenor sings so melodramatically, ". . . Guadalajara, Guadalajara (crescendo), Guadalajara . . ." like it's fucking paradise.

Anyhow, the three of us conspirators—me doubling over in pain and tired from the debilitating heroin I had snorted last night, Andrew, trying to be cool—cool fool sitting on a hill, and Ted, wondering if his goddam ass is covered—we call Aero Cargo and discover that the package was indeed there, but we need 700 pesos or $56 to cover the taxes. For a minute I feel a huge, uncontrollable wave of paranoia overtake me and I want out—out of this bullshit riff of waiting and never knowing if we're being watched—and you know the ol' story—if you get busted overseas, you're in for the hassle of your life—and Mexico, for all intents and purposes, is definitely overseas. And I want to run away and forget my $4,000, and my arms with track marks all over them, and the man I supposedly loved, who lived in a world of pipe dreams. But only for a minute because I knew I was in too far. So Ted scrapes together about 300 pesos and some French francs from Morocco and we all pile into the Safari and head for town to cash a check and I get the eeriest feeling that someone is watching me—but Andrew assures me that it's only paranoia creeping up—and to keep my disease to myself because paranoia is a disease—a communicable one—you have it and to get rid of it you pass it on, brother. And on the way into town Ted explains that the so-called package is, in reality, 250 kilos of hash built into an armoire. And it should weigh 500 pounds altogether, he was a few pounds short—and he sent it out himself and there is glass in the doors and intricate carvings all over. Well—we three ain't dummies—and we know we can't haul the armoire in a Safari jeep, so we hurriedly head for José Cortezar father's mattress factory. There we find José passed out and green, nodded out under a tree. "Hey brother" (brother my ass), "we need you for a leetle while." And Andrew and Teddy explain to José that a package has come in—they don't need to explain what it is—he nods—and a smile slips on his face—he too gets turned on by the idea of smuggling— sure, man—he will get a truck and four of his father's workers to help us unload it. Smuggling is like a drug in itself. The excitement and the fear get you as stoned, if not more so, as any drug. I always had the Mata Hari complex. Suddenly, I just don't want to be around. I want to go to the beach and swim and lie in the sun— but Ted insists that I go—just to keep it in the family . . . again, paranoia, please brother—ol' misery sure 'nough loves its company. So we meet José at the casa—me in a tiny top and cut-offs, Andrew in his hat and Ted in his pants and shirt—we make tracks for the office of Aero Cargo in José's truck. I really didn't want to be there, and I pray to whomever may be there listening to get me out of this. At Aero Cargo there is an overabundance of workers and *hombres* but we walk with our heads held high—no pun intended—I mean we were on top of the world—temporarily, man, so temporarily. Everyone is staring so hard at us—and I know that Ted is trying to avoid being noticed—he keeps to the paneling of the office wall, leaving Andrew to pick up the package, which is in his name. Andrew pays the taxes—he is sweating so much now—and I take his hand, because I know that he is weak, and trying so hard not to show it. And Ted is very businesslike as José and his four helpers lift up the extraordinarily heavy package and put it on the truck. Suddenly Ted panics and whispers to me, "Susan, it's a goddam new crate it's in—I packed the armoire and it wasn't in that crate—it's brand new, I never saw it before," as if I can come up with the answers. This debonair businessman, this big-time con artist turns absolutely beige and really, I mean this is no joke, I wish that I had a picture—his hair stands up and he really looks like a goddam chicken with his beaked nose. I say, "Hey man, let's pass on this deal and leave the friggin' dope here until we can figure it out." But greed triumphs as usual as Ted decides, well, maybe the Mexicans broke the crate and had to make a new one. Because he assures me, sweat on the backs of his hands, the package never went through the U.S. Customs, but directly from Tangier to Mexico and after all, what can we do now? Andrew is too busy helping José to notice the newness of the crate and Ted neglects to tell him. I mean, after all, who is Andrew except the flunky who will bear all the responsibility if anything happens, because the package is in his name? And we wave good-by to all the people at the Aero Cargo office, not realizing that about one-quarter of them are police. The drive back to the apartment is very quiet—except for José who chatters all the way, stoned and ignorant of the situation. I guess ignorance might be bliss after all.

Once we return to the apartment, all the workers and José and Andrew have the unenviable task of uncrating the armoire and bringing it up the steps. Ted and I run ahead—throw out all the grass in the apartment but two joints, which I hide in my make-up case along with two mandrax. We stash the cocaine and household heroin in silver foil high in the closet, where I imagine it still is. Then I make fruit salad for lunch and snort the cocaine we left out. The armoire finally comes into the apartment. Four tired Mexican peons, one now definitely exhausted José Cortezar, one pooped-out Andrew, and the metadirector Ted deposit one of the most beautiful pieces of furniture I have ever seen in our living room. I give tall glasses of lemonade to all the workers and thank José, who is leaving for Ensenada in two hours. He flies out the door, and finally Andrew and I collapse in the middle of the floor with Ted pacing up and down, looking suspiciously out the window.

The armoire is a fine example of the lost art of woodcarving. It's about nine feet tall and five feet wide and the front of it is carved delicately with small figures, deer and goats. And I say to Ted, "Where the hell is the hash?" And he smiles to himself and walks over to the armoire looking more calm and less like a scared rabbit, because he is back in his role of he-man-adventurer smuggler. We stand on a chair and I see that the whole top and bottom of the armoire are false, full of hidden shit—so to speak. Suddenly, Ted turns green again, his hair stands up like little blades of dried-out grass and he whispers, "Someone goddam opened this, I can tell—it's not the finished color of the armoire. Now it all fits, the unfamiliar crating and the smiling Mexicans and I'm getting the fuck out of here." Filled with fear, he thinks only of himself—and gentle Andrew poor soul, he is cool, man, and not to be daunted in his hour of triumph, he says, "Hey man, relax, we both know that the package never went through U.S. Customs, and if they had wanted to bust us we would never have received the package." And me, free me, I have to pee fast and remember the day, two years long gone, when Ivan and I were met by the F.B.I. and I cry because as I try to put everything in context and remember, I have the electrifying realization that soon I will only remember. I stay in the bathroom a long time, feeling myself marooned. It's June, and I feel another lousy riff coming on. And as I walk back into the other room I hear Ted droning on, ". . . and man I've seen too many TV shows and I know the trip—get hip—if they want us, we are right now surrounded—they're only waiting for us to open up the panels and remove the hash. So let's get out of this place—maybe they'll forget our faces. Also, remember, Andrew and Susan, they can't get us for something that we didn't do, for all we know the package was a gift to Andrew from a friend in Morocco—and we're cool (cool fool sitting on a hill) since we have no idea what's in the armoire." And the chicken putters into the other room and says he wants to make reservations to leave that night—and I have the disease (paranoia) bad—I say to Andrew, "Honey I'm scared that they have us. Let's go to town and make reservations to leave (why the fuck aren't I at the beach?) and stay away until we feel that the vibes are O.K." And Andrew chuckles and languorously stretches out without a single doubt, like he's home free, and says to me, "Baby, you and your paranoid buddy Ted (my buddy?), you two fly out of here tonight and I'll stay here for a few days to make sure that everything is fine—go and get your passport and visa and open ticket—we'll drive to town, make reservations, and you'll be safe in L.A. tonight." I start to think, something here stinks, why wouldn't he let me go yesterday. But at this point, ladies and gents, I went to collect my papers, follow my instincts, and split. I was so nervous I never even put shoes on—I took one mandrax to cool myself down—pulled my hair back, and in cut-offs and a little top (as usual) headed for the car with Andrew and Ted. The mandrax was just starting to take its effect and the three of us walked to the jeep. Ted—almost visibly shaking, got in the back, Andrew got in the driver's seat, and (did I remember to lock the door?) I was just climbing into my seat when I looked up and saw a huge Mexican, about six-two, with a mustache, a sombrero, and a machine gun—and I looked at Andrew and he looked at me and I looked at him and he looked at me and I said out loud, "Do you believe this?" And suddenly there were thirty Mexican police. It was hard to tell exactly how many since all of them were *Federales* not dressed in uniforms; and thirty machine guns and pistols and the heat, and I'm getting thrown against a car and being frisked (a little stoned by now, yelling "Hey man, what the fuck do you think do you think you're doing?"), but no one understood English and handcuffs on *Senor* Andrew—the package was in his name and someone in God's name help me—keep it cool on the outside Susan—I mean really, what is going on? And an older man, maybe forty-five or so with a mustache and a .38 revolver asks me (Jesus—it seemed like everyone in town had gathered around our apartment building and was watching—screaming) for the key—and I don't want to go into my purse because I have grass there—keep cool—God help me to hold onto my purse—and it was like a goddam movie—the police acted like we were Bonnie and Clyde. And they break down the door—and all this Spanish talk and pandemonium and four of the big *Federales* push Ted (who has totally blown it and is hysterical by now and whispers to me "Don't tell them a thing, cry, act inno-cent—ask them why are they here?"), and I remember the joints in my purse, however, at this point I'm stoned on my downer and bel-ligerent as hell—and two of the *hombres* identify themselves as American F.B.I. men and casually say to me, "Congratulations, girlie—you are part of the first hash bust ever in the Baja—and you're in for the longest and hottest summer of yer life." Andrew is handcuffed and crying, "Honey, I'm sorry, I know you've seen this movie before." I can't cry, but as I watch the four *Federales* take hatchets and break into the armoire on the top and the bottom look-ing for the dope I maneuver my hand into my purse, unzip my make-up case—keeping my eyes on as many of the cops as I can—slip out the two joints and mandrax and stash the joints behind the pillows of the sofa. At least they can't grab me for possession—so I thought! And no one sees me—only Andrew and he winks at me. The sweat is pouring off his face now, and since he is handcuffed and unable to wipe it off he asks me to. As I do, the older gentle-man asks me if I know what is coming out of the armoire in kilo bags (only the best hash he'll ever see), and I say no—and another man—this one older, less fluent in English, and definitely more belligerent-looking, is checking out Ted's arms for needle marks. Ted never had the guts to shoot a B-B gun, let alone dope—and I wonder if this is it for me, with enough track marks on my arms to sponsor a roller derby, but he sees only deep tan and some rather large black-and-blue marks—and a man who identifies himself, amid all the noise of hachets and yelling, as the district prosecutor of Baja—he looks at me rather softly and says, "Susan (how the hell does he know my name unless they have been watching me?), Susan, do you know how serious this is?" And I hostilely spit out, "I don't know what's going on here, what is this all about?" (He's now going through my clothes—at least the house is clean of drugs.) "I de-mand my rights." And he asks me why I don't cry and I answer that I have nothing to fear, I am innocent. Meanwhile, the two American F.B.I. motherfuckers are telling me that I have to give them the name of someone to call in the States for me because I won't be able to get near a phone, and anyway the lines are never working—and I say no—I don't need help—I'm protected, my good karma will get me out—and one says to Andrew, "O.K., Buster, who should we call for her?" and Andrew gives them my parents' phone number and for the first time I feel fears well up because they can't possibly go through this again. The apartment is now in a shambles—the drawers are on the floor—the clothes are everywhere—the music and books all over—I can't bear the pain. The district prosecutor tells us to go to the car now—we are being taken to jail. So we are marched down the stairs and they try to handcuff me and (still hostile from my downer) I kick out—and they laugh—I see one of many *policía* pocket my locket, given to me by my father on my sixth birthday and inscribed "To Susan Beth," and I scream out at this thief, but no one cares. I am just another prisoner without rights and there are hundred of Mexicans looking for action gathered outside our house. I see Mr. Cortezar in the corner, shaking his head, Oh, the gossip now, and I wonder where José is, but my thoughts are interrupted by the friggin' F.B.I. man telling me that in Mexico you are guilty until proven innocent. Andrew, Ted, and I are shown into a yellow VW, I can't believe they put us together. Ted says, "Baby, keep your mouth tight. We'll get you out of here—you just don't know a thing." Andrew tells me not to worry, the brothers will get us out—and we do have such good karma. This reality crashed down so quickly—good-by you dreamers, good-by—the realities sure do change. There is a great disparity between the dream and the fact.

The drive to the jail is short; everything is very close in La Paz. The jail, or Edificio M. Sobarzo, is an old hospital with thick walls and a lot of police hanging around outside. They take us out of the car at gunpoint, it is around four o'clock now, and I scream for Andrew to come with me. He is dragged away and the district prosecutor takes my purse and finally looks through—stops and takes out my make-up case, now empty of drugs. He then looks over my diary and I get weak in the knees—all my notes about methedrine madness and heroin. He confiscates it and I am led to a cell isolated from the rest of the jail. There are at least thirty male eyes following me—the cell they lead me to looks very small—perhaps it is a single cell for me alone. I start to panic as they open up the huge barred door and push me into a dark hole—good-by sunlight, good-by dark-eyed girl, you were so free so free, and the door swings shut with me wondering what in the fuck is going on.

*T*he jailhouse riff is not a humorous part of the narrative. It was tragic then, and in retrospect makes me feel slightly pathetic and somewhat amazed. Somehow, somewhere, I found reservoirs of strength that enabled me to keep myself from going completely mad. When the cell door shut, I found myself in a hole about fifteen by six feet, very dark, dank, and filthy. However, the one saving grace of my cell was that the very thick stone walls kept it relatively cool. There was a door with a huge lock in the middle of the back wall. I thought it maybe led to a torture chamber, having no idea what I was in for. After I had been busted, the kindly F.B.I. man had whispered in my ear for me to remove my earrings—because you never know, I mean, they might rip them off. This was never to come to pass, it was probably just the asshole's way of lording it over me. I looked around the room and saw a cement slab about halfway down one wall that served as a cool place to lie down, a broken-down table, no windows, needless to say, and a bed. However, my ecstasy at discovering a place to rest was short-lived, because the bed consisted of about fifty-year-old box springs, and a cover filled with lice and roaches. I noticed a huge spider climbing the wall. I walked into the so-called bathroom and stopped dead in my tracks, horrified for the tenth time that day. For starters, the stench was unbearable. I mean this wasn't the Guadalajara Hilton. There was no toilet, merely a hole in the floor—no sink or shower, just a small faucet. But the most upsetting factor was that although I had thought I was alone, in the corner there was a woman in a long, nondescript dress, pregnant, who sat on the floor holding her knees. Her face was Mongoloid, she couldn't speak, and was apparently severely retarded. She sat there, in this huddle, with a few scroungy boxes around her: these contained her clothes and some old bread. I was panic-stricken; I spoke no Spanish and if she proved to be violent, I had no way to communicate with her or even to call for help, since the guards had disappeared. I had to go to the bathroom very badly, but aside from there being no toilet and the appalling sanitary conditions, there was no way that I would go with her around. Due to this fear, I didn't go for two and a half days. The incongruous aspect of Juanita, as I later discovered was her name, was the fact that she had hung a clothesline in the bathroom to hang up the clothes she had washed in dirty water. She was determined, in her foggy notion of things, to remain clean, even in her perilous situation, and despite the fact that the dampness never permitted anything to dry. I walked out of the bathroom with her eyes following me carefully and sat down on the floor, in front of the cell door. From this vantage point I could see a large and beautiful flowering tree in front of the cell. The huge wall to the right of my cell bounded the men's side and had a guard atop it; out on the street, a few *policía* wandered to and fro. I would adopt the tree as my own, because it was the only sign of free and growing life that I could see.

What in God's name was I going to do? I had no idea if they could hold us and I had no money except for fifty pesos, and no recourse to any action. I judged the time to be about 5:30 or so and I saw a group of about thirty policemen marching back toward my cell—Oh my God—a gang rape, not unlike what the F.B.I. man had said. I mean if they could rip my earrings out of my ears—they could do anything. Who would ever know what had happened? But the police stopped directly beside my tree, lined up, and the drill sergeant started yelling out commands, I mean they were drilling— a step to the right, two to the left, about face, and at each turn I could see a few eyes looking at me suspiciously—the *gringita*. The police apparently ranged in age from eighteen to sixty, were all sizes, all shapes, and not very tough. As Andrew had told me, a policeman had the highest paying civil job—and this alone attracted most of the men. The sun was setting behind the tree and I knew that the ocean lay in that direction. Suddenly, from behind my cell and through the door I had noticed I heard pounding on the wall and yelling, yelling, louder yelling, enough to scare me. Who was back there? Maybe the male prisoners, maybe Andrew. I ran and started pounding the huge metal door and screaming "Andrew!" And the louder I pounded, the louder they did, until I was crying and screaming and pounding and working myself up to a frenzy, and then my cell door swung open and four *policía* walked in and I felt my knees start to shake and they looked at me quizzically and they motioned me aside and I moved back. The largest policeman took a giant key from his chain and opened the metal door. I rushed forward to see if Andrew was there and was grabbed by a small policeman with a mustache, who looked kindly at me with his huge brown eyes, as if to say, I'm so sorry, *señorita,* and I tried to question the police as to who was behind the door; however, no one understood English, and I thought what a dummy I was for never learning Spanish. The little fat tender policeman pointed at his head and made the universal circle motion that means crazy—and I got pissed and thought he meant me, but when I saw behind the door I saw an older man in a Yankee baseball team T shirt and a baseball cap. He said in English, "Me Tony," and I saw he had on old Bermuda shorts, and then he started to sing the Mexican hat dance and was accompanied by a very old man dressed in, of all things, a Mickey Mouse T shirt, and he had no eyes and Tony yelled, "Felix him," and the little guard made the crazy sign again and I realized that the crazy or mentally unbalanced prisoners were locked up behind me, and the thought unnerved me. The police locked up the door again and left—their nightly check over—and looked at me as they exited. I was left alone with the pregnant retarded woman and darkness came.

I was starving and huddled on the floor, afraid of the lice in the bed—it was chilly, still May, and the evenings were breezy, the stars outside my cell thick. In tropical places the sky is so heavy that it looks as if you can touch the stars. It was so quiet and peaceful, like every other evening in La Paz, that it calmed me down slightly; it was hard to believe that it was so peaceful in a prison. My legs had goose bumps all over and I felt nauseous—I thought it was from the heroin the night before. Suddenly I heard a radio come on very loudly and a rapid Spanish voice droning on and on—the news—and then my own name, Susan Beth Nadler, followed by Andrew's name and Ted's; I realized that we were indeed big news. I was to hear my name every hour that night and the next day until I thought they were talking about someone else. Around 7:30 or so the afternoon guard, a young boy with barely enough hair for a mustache, opened up the cell, turned on the single, glaring bulb, and handed me a paper plate with fried fish and potatoes on it, a plastic fork, and a blanket. Was this the prison food? Did they have special food for the women? He looked at me and said, *"Señor* José Cortezar." I thought that José had found out about us and sent me food. Then the guard left. I put the blanket on the floor in front of the cell door and looked at the food, knowing I could never eat it; then I walked into the bathroom and saw the woman huddled on the floor and I put the food on one of her boxes. She never moved and I wondered if she knew what was happening. I sat on the blanket now, turned off the bulb, and wondered what was to happen. I missed Andrew so much that I started to cry, and the goddam news came on and José's name was mentioned and I realized that they had picked him up too, poor innocent José. What would happen to him with his previous record? (Then again, what would happen to me if it were known that I had a previous record?) His father had totally blown any chance of respectability in that town. We had not only lost our money, the hash, wasted our time, and probably ruined our lives, but we had also ruined the lives of people who had tried to be nice to us, never suspecting that we were in fact manipulating them. Oh, why hadn't I been at the beach that day? But I knew the answers to my questions lay much deeper than that. So I gazed at the stars and took out my little address book and pen, just so I wouldn't forget it, and, I see now, to restate and reinforce my sanity. I copied out the words to two songs Andrew and I had written. We had had such high hopes, and now look.

My memories were just starting to overwhelm me when the light in the bathroom went on and I heard singing. Jesus. Juanita came floating through the cell, naked—her long, stringy, black hair floating behind her and her thin, black-nippled breasts swinging, her pregnancy huge and somehow comforting. She danced and sang as if she didn't see me, which she probably didn't—and hummed to herself as she so gracefully choreographed her own special dance of joy and impending motherhood. She wove her way back into the bathroom and sat the tired red bucket under the faucet and sang to the droplets that slowly fell into her hands. Apparently night was the only time water came out of the faucet, and she produced a small bit of soap from her hand and washed herself, always singing, until she was clean. She used her dress for a towel, and combed her hair with her fingers. Then she shyly walked up to me and offered me the soap, which I refused. She shook her head, danced back, put on another nondescript dress, turned out the light, and huddled into her corner to fall asleep. (She was to repeat this eerie and somehow religious dance every evening at approximately the same time, with the same song and dance, until she was taken away, half-crazed with pain, to have her child.) I wondered who the father was. I didn't have much time to wonder because shortly after she went to sleep, four of the *Federales* who had been present at my bust came to get me: heading them was the tall, mustached man they called Adolfo—the first person I had looked up and seen when I was busted. They were all armed with machine guns, as if I were a criminal, which I guess I was. They marched me up to a VW bus and pointed to me that I was to get in. Was this it? Was I being freed? Had someone decided that it was all a big mistake?

We drove practically to the center of town. I recognized a restaurant where Andrew and I had eaten many times. The van stopped, the door was opened by police, and Adolfo—apparently the head man—took my hand and helped me down. I saw maybe thirty-five men in a small room with bright lights. I wouldn't move, but

Adolfo pulled me into the room and pointed out a seat for me in front of a huge desk and the elderly man with the mustache I recognized from the afternoon, who had known my name and identified himself as the district prosecutor of Baja. I also saw the man who had checked my arms for marks, the F.B.I. men, and several photographers. A newspaper reporter with a press badge and camera winked at me. They could shove it up their asses, there was no way I was going to let them photograph me. I thought of my parents—briefly—the F.B.I. man walked up to me and I felt his sneaky presence—it was slimy, unhealthy. He had on a big knife and as my eyes rested on it he grabbed it—like, to scare me. Big-time, he was probably trying to prove his goddam virility with his knife—the ol' cops-and-robbers number. Only this time I had been caught. He said, "Listen Susan, I have three things to tell you. Firstly, I'm going to call your parents tomorrow when I leave for San Diego. Secondly, cooperate with these people, let them take your picture. This man here is the district prosecutor, he is going to interrogate you, be helpful. And finally," he moved closer as if to establish a secret rapport with me, "if you tell me everything about Andrew and Ted, or get Andrew to confess, I promise you you'll be out of here in two days, deported home with no problems." Jesus, the old cop story, rat on a friend. I would never fall for that one. I kindly informed him that no one was taking my picture, click, click, in the background. I gave the newspaperman the finger and covered my face. I told the F.B.I. man that I was happy that he would call my parents, but that I had no idea what was going on, and that turning in your friend was a little passé. He was surprised, said he had thought a smart gal like me would cooperate, and that he hoped I'd stay in jail for thirty years. They would probably sentence me for that long, since they had never seen hash before in Baja. I mean even I knew that Mexico was strictly a grass country (that was one thing I certainly knew). "Good-by Susan, and I hope that they get you." Oh, thanks a lot for trying to help me. You low-life narc.

He walked away, and I never saw him again; but he did call my parents and broke the news to them very gently. The interrogation now started, and the newspaperman was asked to leave, but the camera finally caught a picture of me. I was very tan, my hair was pulled back, and since my passport had been reissued in Jerusalem, the newspaper never quite got my story right, and featured headlines that I was from India, a spy, and liked only sex and drugs; I mean, couldn't you tell that from the picture? There was an interpreter present, a fat woman who worked for the judge, who later gave all the information to my lawyer; he nicknamed her "the fat connection." Very funny, yeah. The district prosecutor would question me, she would interpret it, and I would answer it in English— she would interpret for him, he would comment on it, and she would type it up. A typically slow but unavoidable situation that lengthened a short process into four hours.

I was informed of my rights, which were few, and told that as far as the district prosecutor was concerned I was guilty—at least until proven innocent. The first questions were very basic, my name, age, height, weight, and nationality. I told them I was American, even though my passport had been reissued in Jerusalem. They thought, cool, man, now we have the whole situation: Jerusalem is in Morocco and she sent out the hash—but this is wrong, man, and we bickered over this point. Again, I don't know where I got the clarity of mind, but I knew that my statements that evening were very important and would form the basis of my defense. Maybe the heat in the office slowed me down, but I thought out each answer. I was charged with possession, acquisition, importation, and transportation of 250 kilos of opium. Not only was I amazed at all the charges, but wary not to correct their mistaken use of the word opium; I mean I had never seen drugs before—so how would I know the difference between hash and opium? No, I did not know and still didn't know that Andrew was smuggling drugs. All I knew was that he had been waiting for a package, a present from a friend in Morocco—whose name I didn't know. Did I know that the armoire contained hash? Obviously not, I had never seen hash before. The only reason I knew that drugs were in the armoire was because the F.B.I. men had told me as the *Federales* broke into it. Andrew

43

worked for a construction company. How the hell did I know where he got his money from? Did *his* wife ask him where the money came from? No answer, smart move.

I knew that Andrew had received a telegram from Aero Cargo on May 23—nothing more. Yes, we lived quite well—Andrew had money (so had I about two months ago). The reason I had my passport and visa and ticket in my purse when I had been picked up was because I was very ill and was leaving La Paz to go to L.A. and see a doctor. No, I was hardly going to L.A. to set up connections for the hash since I didn't even know there was hash in the furniture. (They kept forgetting that point.) Yes, I thought that Andrew was a legitimate businessman, I had gone with him to see realtors in La Paz to try and make connections for his company's land-development business. The company was planning to build hotels in Baja. Ted was not an architect and I wasn't that into the business end of things. Now, we were not married but had very serious plans. Yes, I had met Ted once in L.A. (the fucker Ted came up smelling like a rose). No, Andrew and I did not use drugs. No, José Cortezar was only a friend. I didn't know if he knew anything or not, since *I* didn't know anything. The reason I went to the Aero Cargo office with Andrew is because he asked me to—I had wanted to go to the beach. At this point the district prosecutor told me I would have been a lot better off at the beach—I thought, "He's telling me." Did I know that José Cortezar was under arrest and in jail as an accomplice? Jesus Christ, I didn't know that, but sure as I could be I thought that José was innocent. How could I know who the connections were? —I didn't even know what was going on.

Yes I had a B.A. degree in Humanities—English Literature (didn't I look educated?). I got my degree from Jerusalem and I spoke a little Arabic, Hebrew, and read French. Yes, I did have a family. Two younger sisters, and my father had his own business and if they would only let me call my parents they would see that all this was a big mistake. Yes, I'd like a Coke (a real Coke). They informed me that the next afternoon they would take me, me alone, back to the apartment where I could get my things, some clothes, some food, the tape deck, records, anything I needed. The district prosecutor also told me that my cell was the only accommodation for women—the only women who ever were in jail were prostitutes and the longest time was for fifteen days—so there were no other cells. Normally they threw all the prostitutes in one cell, treating them like the animals they thought they were. No, there was no food, and don't ask any more questions. I finished off by declaring my innocence and was escorted back to the van at gunpoint, arrived at my cell at 2:30 A.M. I grabbed my blanket, put it on the floor in front of the cell door, and listened to the guards yell at each other, "Julio," "*Sí,* Adolfo," and the news, my cigarette burning. Juanita turned over in her sleep, Tony and the other loonies screamed in their sleep, I was cold and dirty. I thought for a moment of collecting some water in a bucket, but decided against it—so dirty. The sun came up, but I couldn't see it—the doorway faced the west, not the east. At 6:00 A.M. the four guards stumbled over me and looked in on the loonies; the prisoners apparently are locked up from 6:00 P.M. to 6:00 A.M. and then can wander about their courtyards. The roosters crowed out Ac-a-pul-cooooo and I had never felt worse in my life. My feet were filthy, my halter top stunk, and my cut-offs were stretched and baggy.

Suddenly a man dressed in civilian clothes and accompanied by a guard appeared at the cell door, just as the other guards left. He was obviously Mexican, but spoke perfect English. He said, "Susan, I am Ernesto Duran, trusty of the prison—don't ask me any questions, I have no time to answer—just listen, I will come later tonight and bring you food from Andrew—he sends his love and tells you everything is or will be all right. I will get permission for you to call your parents later. Your trial will be in two days—don't cry or worry, it will help or change nothing. Today you will be taken back to your apartment to get your things. Andrew says for you to take all you can. There is a lawyer coming down from Andrew's people tomorrow, he got the call a little while ago." (How did the news travel so quickly to L.A.? They must have called that apartment to find out how things were coming and heard from Mr. Cortezar.) "Now you take care, I will bring you a valium tonight, don't worry." And he left with me wondering what in the hell a trusty was, and who the lawyer was, and what I would say to my parents. I had a feeling that all these problems would be over soon; I never believed that anything could really happen to me—I was part of the Pepsi Generation—free and glamorous.

*J*ail day two was mighty blue. I
kept thinking this is only a dream, but it was about 8:30 in the
morning and I was definitely not free to leave. I could feel myself
clearly now and when I put out my cigarette it was on a cold stone
floor. The guards apparently changed every twelve hours, one tour of
duty lasting from 6:00 A.M. to 6:00 P.M. and another from evening
to morning. I had eaten nothing for a day and yet I wasn't hungry,
everything was so lifeless in the cell, the cold stone, the flat lighting, the odors. Juanita slept on in the bathroom, curled silently on
the slimy floor. I began to pace up and down and tried to think of
ways to occupy myself. I didn't want to admit defeat, but I was
busted, the dream was definitely over, or at least interrupted. Despair was my only companion, as close and real to me as Harry Karma
had been in the past. Despair because I was caught in a situation
where I was no longer in control. It is necessary to be in a position
to work with life instead of being worked over by life. So despair and
I, we finally cried, and I remember crying for many hours.

The older man who was my guard now opened the cell door for
one minute. I wanted to run, but there was no benefit in running.
La Paz is like an island surrounded by water on three sides, with
Tijuana as its upper border. Where could I go anyway? The old
guard sat on the edge of the bed and he offered me his handkerchief.
Then he went into his wallet and pulled out an article from the
newspaper, a very long article and I looked at the pictures he

showed me and saw my own face peering back at me. It was the story of Andrew and Ted and me, so I surmised, but was never sure. He wanted to cheer me up and show me that I had made the newspapers. I cried harder. The old guard laughed quietly, out of discomfort or evil, I never knew. I imagine he had known desperation too. He left my cell and I remained on the floor crying, for several hours. I had almost cried myself to sleep, nodding out as peacefully as if I were back at the apartment in bed with Andrew, when I glanced up and saw a very dirty young man standing and staring at me. I was too weak to be belligerent, as I would have been two days ago. Instead I wondered at the gentleness of his smile and the grease on his hands and clothes. He seemed to be dressed like a mechanic. He smiled at me again and brusquely (although he couldn't disguise his genuine concern) motioned to me that I should wipe away the tears. He called me Susana, so he must have heard about me on the radio. He put his hand into his back pocket and produced two mangoes which he slipped through the bars to me. Why, I wondered, was he interested in me unless he was just a sensation seeker or a policeman. Then he looked behind him, as if to check for the guards, and pulled a small cross, made from abalone shell, out of his breast pocket. He tried to give it to me, and I didn't know what to do. He repeated over and over again, Jesús Cristo, Jesús Cristo, and I understood he wanted his god to be with me and somehow help me. I took the cross from his hands and he just kept smiling and smiling; then he turned around, saw the old guard approaching, and left quickly. He would return early every morning the remainder of my time in jail—he became a part of the order of my day, with the fruit, ice cream, and religion he brought. Later he would bring his mother and father, so poor, to try to help me with tortillas and religion. The poor Mexicans are by far the kindest and most tender people I have ever known. They have endless sympathy for the underdog and I was definitely the underdog of the season in Baja that year. I had lived in La Paz with Andrew for six weeks before the bust and I had never bothered to get to know any of the people; we had always existed in our own small world. The doors to that world were to open up and admit many new people; I had just missed them before.

There was so much I had missed. Some days, when depression became overbearing and I could not overcome it, my joy of life was revitalized instantly by a mango from Tommy, or a compassionate joke, only partly understood, in Spanish, from one of my guards. Somehow these people went directly to the heart of life. They avoided the obvious desperation of a situation. Possibly it was because so much of their lives was lived in desperation; desperation because they had no money to send their children to college or even feed them, desperation because they could never speak freely about their government. Many of my friends in the U.S., in our desperation to be political, had missed the point that there is not the desperation in this country that exists in so many others. We are a spoiled generation of takers. The poor of Mexico had a respect for life and an ability to instill joy into the most mundane events and conversations. Their joy in having food, in a good joke, in the rainfall, far outdistanced their desperation over money, They had learned to find joy where so many found boredom. Most importantly, they had learned to share their joy. How had I missed them? I was too concerned about taking. A sybaritic daughter of the sixties, I never had the time.

I couldn't fully appreciate the message the boy brought me, because about fifteen minutes after the visit, as I sat on the cool floor and devoured my mangoes, wiping my hands on my cut-offs, the cell door opened and the district prosecutor stood there, hands on his hips. "You must eat more, Susana." (Why don't you eat shit?). "You must take care not to drink the water from the bathroom. You will get sick. I cannot come in—the smell is too bad. You come out here, under this small tree. A car will take you to your apartment for your things. Juanita, the crazy one in the bathroom, she is harmless, raped by her own father—now, hurry Susana." The hot air hit me again as I ran outside. Two *Federales* with machine guns were waiting for me under the beautiful blossoming tree. They tipped their sombreros to me, I tipped my finger to my nose; however, they missed that. The district prosecutor looked very clean in his freshly pressed white shirt and chinos. The two *Federales* smelled of soap and lavender water, I smelled of urine and tears. One thing I will say for the Baja brigade, they were compulsively clean. Perhaps because of the intense heat, they were more conscious of odors. None of these men ever walked into my cell, the smell was too much for them. This says a lot (or a little) about the Mexican penal system. Mexicans regard women as possessions who belong at home cooking, cleaning, caring for the children; if a woman is a prostitute, well, she is no longer considered a woman, because when respect goes, so does humane treatment. The jail conditions for the prostitute were equivalent to her social standing. The district prosecutor said, "Oh Susana, if only your mother and father could see their eldest daughter now, they would be so ashamed." (They would kill me.) "Come, let us go to your apartment and collect some things for you and your boys, so that you may be a little more comfortable." I had been in jail less than twenty-four hours, but the shock of being in the daylight was overwhelming. We drove in the district prosecutor's car, my thighs stuck to the plastic seat covers. I started wondering if the F.B.I. men had indeed contacted my parents. I would rather have stayed in jail for five years than face my parents; busted this second and more serious time, I was in a very degrading position.

We drove up to my apartment and I inwardly winced. The doors were boarded shut and the windows too. We climbed the steps; myself, the district prosecutor, and the police went in. The place was unrecognizable as my former abode. Everything was on the fucking floor—dishes, clothes, papers, songs, my heart, my lies, and my hopes. I really didn't know where to begin or what to take. I wanted to take a shower, but the district prosecutor told me, "It is against the regulations, Susan." (Screw you, you are the regulations, you should make an exception for me.) I first collected my underwear, to the astonishment of the two *Federales* who giggled— what's the matter, haven't they ever seen bikini underpants made out of the American flag? I hadn't brought much with me to La Paz, so I put everything in my bag and got Andrew's clothes, and put them in his luggage. Ted's three-piece suit would be a big hit in the cell. I packed it in his overnight case.

My bathroom trip was perhaps the funniest. I stood there collecting Elizabeth Arden make-up remover, moisturizers, Shalimar perfume, razors, and as the D.P. suggested, Tampax. He obviously thought I would be there a lot longer than I did. I avoided taking my herbal laxative, Innerclean, I wouldn't want the runs in jail. I closed the door in their faces and sat down on the toilet—the cleanest thing I'd seen in a long time. No sooner had I started to pee when I heard the D.P. yelling, "No suicide Susana." I answered, "All I want to do now . . ." Now what would be a ladylike reply? But I guess with him standing next to the door, he heard the answer. Where in my cell would I put all this stuff? I walked out, everyone was relieved, and I collected about twenty tapes—good ol' Joni Mitchell, James Taylor, Jackson Brown, and Roberta Flack. I also took my recorder and Andrew's guitar, but who knew when we would use them again? The D.P. suggested that I take all the stuff off the walls, like the mandalas would blend in with the décor of spiders in my cell. Little did he know that the Krishna band had originally come in another shipment of hash—our joke on him. I also took cups and knives and forks and rugs—the Mexicans believe in traveling with your possessions wherever you go. The fruit salad from the day before sat wilted on the table. We left the apartment and I took one last, longing look around. Good-by yesterday of love and squalor and false dreams of dollars. Oh, the damage done!

Once back at the jail, my parcels had to be examined by the *alcaide*—the warden. I was escorted into an office, which was large and like a waiting-rrom at a hospital, which is exactly what the room had been when the building was a hospital. It was very disorganized—I saw one phone and behind it a little table, the door leading to the office of the *comandante* of the jail. His presence loomed like a character from the wild west. I couldn't understand: if he wasn't a warden, what *was* a *comandante*? The warden himself turned out to be an old man, perhaps sixty-five or so, with a small shrunken face, a small shrunken sombrero, and the worst B.O. of any human being I have ever encountered. Normally things like that don't bother me, but this little man with heavy alcohol on his breath and a distant twinkled-out winkle in his stoned eye—he *smelled*. He also spoke no English and so our conversations were limited. He took all of Andrew's and Ted's things and rapped the guard on duty on the back. The jail looked like a huge complex to me; I couldn't tell where the men were kept. Later Andrew explained that he and Ted were kept in a big general "hole" for the first week along with thirty or so drunks. There were no toilet facilities. Later they were moved to private cells. Anyhow, the guard took all the things, winked, the warden giggled, the D.P. sighed, and I was taken back to my cell. Where did my things go?

The cell when I entered stank, I felt nauseous, and realized that I couldn't even vomit in the bathroom because I wouldn't walk in. I was so tired. However, I had managed to take a notebook and the joints and mandrax. I had sneaked them all into my purse at the apartment. The Mexicans never really searched me well—merely cursory feel-ups. I must have been loonier than ever as I sat on the blanket on the floor, watching the sun set behind my newly adopted tree, writing a love note to Andrew and sneaking an occasional hit off a joint—the epitome of self-destruction and loss of values. It I had been caught, I'd still be there: the basis of my defense was that I had never seen dope. I wrote for about an hour to Andrew—about how I loved him still and knew that he had never done anything to hurt me, and about how we would soon be free. I was dazed and stoned out by the time it was close to 6:00 P.M. when I saw Ernesto Duran approach. My heart started to flutter and I started to shake. But he calmed me right down. "Susan, this guard with me understands English pretty well; in a few minutes they will come to get you to call your parents. José Cortezar is in jail too, not in a cell, he is sleeping in the warden's office for questioning. He is sending you food these days. I will slip a valium into your food, tonight, fish sandwich. I am a trusty of the prison, meaning there is more than sufficient confidence in me around here, so I am in charge of dispensing the drugs to the prisoners, translating, plus I can go to town with a guard to buy things, food, etc. Don't interrupt me. Andrew sends his love, they got their clothes and thank you. You will get yours tomorrow. However, you won't get your fork, knife, or tweezers because these idiots are afraid you will try to commit suicide. A lawyer from Andrew's people will be here tomorrow, you will be able to see Andrew and Ted when he comes. Those two are paying off the warden. Be strong. I must go. Andrew says to tell your people you need all the help you can get. Peace and good-by." I begged him to take my note to Andrew, which he did. Thus began our system of note exchange. He was a very strange man to become our friend, but I never trusted him. He had and would continue to have too many asses to lick to become a trusty. I never knew what he would tell or to whom, to help himself. And he was always propositioning either Andrew or me—if a guy can't make up his mind about that, who can trust him? Anyway, things were starting to happen. The guards changed and the young guard, Billy, brought back my clothes and possessions. I decided to hang the mandalas on the walls, and put the Krishna band on the table. I had brought lots of cleaning equipment and began an hour-long scrubbing-down of walls and floors with Juanita alternately laughing and sleeping. Lysol on the floor, in the so-called toilet, on the shelves. I set up my sleeping bag on the bed, so I wouldn't run the risk of rats and have several layers of protection between me and the lice. I had also brought lots of candles and books, which I set next to my bed. All my toiletries went into a straw basket on the table. I planned to join Juanita later that evening in her cleaning ritual. Andrew had given me the tape deck for a while, and I decided to put on Jackson Brown. But just as I switched it on, the guards came to get me and I imagined it was to call my parents. I was very nervous, more nervous about them than even the D.P. I left the cell praying Juanita wouldn't touch anything.

I walked into the night air, which was cooler now, and saw all the stars. I shivered in my bare feet, my hands smelled like Lysol, I had a rag tucked into my cut-offs. The air, to bring me out in the air was necessary, but it taunted me with the life I missed so much already. The office was deserted now and I saw Ernesto being ushered into a door that apparently led to his cell. He pointed to a plate and I saw my fish sandwich. I would absolutely blast him if anyone saw the valium he had slipped in, but what could I really do? I thought to myself: better get over that useless hostility. No one in the office spoke English. I recognized some of the guards that came in at six to check on Tony, Felix, and the dead-end gang that lived in the cells behind me. The guards motioned to the phone and I dialed 01, the long-distance operator for about ten minutes, praying that the lines weren't down today. Pittsburgh seemed so far away and I could imagine my parents, mellow and gentle, and Little Bit, my younger sister with her long black hair and perfect school Spanish. They would be sitting in the living room watching Patches, the eight-year-old poodle, play on the Oriental rug, and Annie the maid would be serving coffee to them. Today was Little Bit's birthday—some present from your older sister. Suddenly, "Hello." "Hello, I have a co-lect call to anyone from Susana." "Yes, operator," my mother said, "we'll accept the charges." And then me sweating so damn hard, "Hello mother, can you hear me?" "Yes, Susan." "Mother, is Daddy there on the other line?" And Little Bit in the background, "She always ruins my birthdays," and Mother, "Yes, Susan, your father's here." She was so short with me and I had mixed emotions, I understood her anger and I wanted sympathy. "Mother, did the F.B.I. man call?" "Yes, Susan," my father said. God, Daddy, I love you so. "He called this morning." "Oh Daddy and Mother, are you mad at me?" "Susan," my mother said, "you're killing yourself and trying to drag us with you." "Oh mother, please, not now." (Screaming, pleading to myself, instant gratification, where are you now?) "Susan," my father said, "the F.B.I. man told us that you were in one hell of a mess, we are going to try to help you." "You're trying to kill your father, Susan." My father, "Susan, we don't know what to do, we are trying to get a hold of one of my friends here, he has a very influential friend there called Manuel. We are going to come down, you picked a hell of a time to get busted, Mexico yesterday received $65 million for drug-control use from the United States. It is a bad time but . . ." My mother, "Why didn't you learn your lesson from Israel, Susan?" (Mother, I wanted to shout, why don't you shut the fuck up, no one down here can ever, ever know I was busted before.) But instead I said, "Mother, please, this is not the time. When will you two be down? I have trial the day after tomorrow." My father, "It's Memorial Day weekend here" (boy, did that seem far away), "the banks are closed, we're going to borrow the money. Just don't get a lawyer yet Susan. Who are these gangsters you're with? The F.B.I. said they were some pretty bad characters." "Oh, Daddy, just Andrew and . . ." The line went dead, as so often happens in La Paz. At least they were coming down, Christ, please give me strength to face them. The end. I was sweating like I had just run three miles and I was starving—the guard gave me back my dinner and I ate it while walking back to my cell, forgetting about the valium, which I scarfed down along with the food.

I entered the cell—it was pitch black and I was petrified. I found matches and lit my candles, the goddam cell looked like a mausoleum with Indian and Tibetan wall hangings and that Krishna band—Oh, play a tune for me! I wanted to scream. Juanita was just waking up for her usual bath. She started to sing and dance and flew out into the cell, naked breasts swinging, scratching her lousy hair. She stopped short and stifled a scream when she saw the candles and my things so neatly arranged. I was standing there naked too, under a huge towel that once had been used for the beach. She kept repeating a word that I later found out meant "church." The cell looked like a mausoleum to me and a church to her. I turned on my radio to try to eliminate some of the weird vibes. I had a cake of soap and a wash rag in my hand and a box of Tide and my dirty clothes in the other. She understood that I wanted to be clean too, and a smile spread across her face, revealing yellow, stumpy teeth. She took my arm and led me into the bathroom and I started to sing with her, who knows what? Just a little da-da-da in any language, it's the same. We waited together as the water droplets started to fall slowly and then more quickly into the bucket. She took the bucket and poured the water on me—it was freezing and I screamed, but grabbed the rag and soap and did the best I could. She watched me and diligently plucked the lice from her hair. Then, as the bucket had filled up again, she poured the freezing water on me and I ran it through my hair, tried to get out the soap, and rinse. I had the chills, but kept on singing as she waited for me to continue the ritual. I collected the water in the bucket and poured it over her—all the time thinking, no one in L.A. would ever believe this. The bathroom stank like crazy, and we sang louder the colder we got. Maybe she wasn't so crazy. I then rinsed her off, grabbed my towel, which had been hung on the line, and dried off, as she dried off with her dress. I waited until more water fell into the bucket, poured a little Tide in, threw in my clothes and decided to soak them for the night. I dried off, felt distinctly cleaner and put on a huge shirt of Andrew's and a pair of jeans, I had lost about seven pounds by then and my jeans hung on me. My hair was soaking with no way for me to dry it. I dove into my sleeping bag, watched as Juanita turned out the light; her singing stopped. I turned the radio off and decided to try to reread parts of *Narcissus and Goldmund*. I fell asleep after seven pages. I awoke with a stiff neck and chills at six o'clock in the morning with four guards staring at the newly decorated cell, and at me in my sleeping bag. My third day in jail was about to begin and prove to be the strangest yet.

I felt sick that entire morning—my hair was still damp and the sleeping bag had been very hot, so I sweated and froze at the same time. The morning was shaky—that is to say that I had slept so soundly that when I awakened I had fully expected to be in bed with Andrew—not on a box spring mattress with spiders, smells, and bars. I tried to exercise, or read, but hadn't the strength for either; however, I picked up a book that I had been reading at the apartment. Someone in L.A. had given it to me some months earlier and I had finally gotten into it. It was a book, not very well known, called *The Ultimate Frontier*, and dealt with such issues as Karma, reincarnation, yoga, higher levels of consciousness, and the ability to maintain this level of consciousness even in an adverse situation. It talks of vegetarianism and belief in the triumph of good over evil, if not in the short run, always in the long run. A primary factor explained in the book is the concept of the Brotherhood of the Light: this organization is composed of souls that never die. It is as if the soul of Moses had never died, merely his physical body. His soul is everlasting or can be reincarnated into various physical shapes. As generations passed his soul evolved more and more. He, Jesus, Krishna, Mohammed, Yogananda, and all the other so-called avatars were sent down to earth to turn man on to the truth and simplicity of God or the Kingdom of Heaven on Earth, which is found within each man, the light of God which shines through every man. They formed a Brotherhood in which their spirits convene and come to the aid of those in need. I had been interested in spiritualism since Jerusalem where I had attempted to study the Cabala. But because a lot of my interest had been in the supernatural, I had believed in a lot of things just to be far out. All those years of intellectual study had lead me into hallucinogenic study of the far-out LSD god, the hidden powers that one had to be an initiate of secret cults to understand. These studies are prevalent in L.A., where everyone has the need to feel that he is part of the chosen, so people form cults. But these power fantasies were no more real than the money I was to get from dope, neither were stable or in my hands. A lot of my personal interest in L.A. had been in phony spiritualism that preached getting high as a way to see God. Its books were about people who found out that they were actually King David this lifetime around; much like my drug-deluded visions of being Cleopatra on the beach in Acapulco. These reinforcements of exterior spiritualism were mainly to aid those who had no internal personal spirit, who couldn't find God without drama or melodrama. These people belie the qualities espoused by the avatars; they are not nice to all their brothers; they go on gigantic ego trips and expect adulation. This is all related to relationships starting from rainbowed reflections in toasters. When you are a desperate human being, you will look into anything and everything for peace of mind. I had always looked outside myself for it, but now I was slowly beginning to see that I had to help myself. So what if I thought I was someone else reincarnated? It weren't goin' to help me get out of jail. No more full on in the divine brother, it's all cool, just go with the flow; it was time for me to understand why I was where I was and how come all the so-called heavies of my generation weren't here to help me. I had only myself to help myself.

With all these thoughts in my mind, I tried to block out all noises and problems. I left jail and despair and myself—I put my mind into absolute silence. I felt like I was floating along myself in a clear, cool world of thoughts—much like meditation described in all the books I had read but never believed necessary for me. I must have sat that way for at least an hour—the first peace of mind or body that I had had in three days, but I was, as always, interrupted. This time it was by Duran, who did it rather gently, being a little respectful of privacy and silence. He announced, "Excuse me Susan, the lawyer from L.A. is here with Andrew and Ted and is waiting to meet you in the hallway—hurry and get changed, girl." I had no time, however, to change my clothes or my head, for the guards were there. I was to see Andrew, I hadn't seen him in three days. They led me barefoot, T-shirted, hair streaming, to the jail proper, and sitting on the benches I spotted Andrew with Ted and another man—apparently our lawyer, who definitely did not look like a representative from the Brotherhood of the Light. Momentarily, all I saw was Andrew and I rushed into his arms and we cried and he looked so thin and he told me I did too and how I wished we were never there, and he promised me that when we got out it would be strictly us on a small farm in the country. We both knew it would never be. I was so carried away that I put my arms around the chicken-face Ted. He was stricken with fear and grief and not bearing up half as well as Andrew. Our time was brief; the warden had been paid off with two bottles of rum so that we could talk before our trial. All the guards were gone.

It was very strange in this anteroom. I was introduced to William Laughlin. Nominally, he was the lawyer for the so-called land-development company back in L.A. He had been sent by the big boys—the ones who supplied Ted with money and connections; they were very businesslike and had meetings in Canada biannually.

I never knew any of them or their names, and I am now very happy that I didn't, and don't. William had gangsterlike overtones, was tall, bearded, and nondescript looking, spiffily dressed in a seersucker suit and polka-dot tie. Andrew whispered to me that he had broken three people out of jail in Mexico so far; one was a guy in for murder at Hermosillo. William had waited until visitors' day, dressed him like a woman, and smuggled him out, in broad daylight. William gathered us under his wing, like a mother hen, and told us that he had arrived the night before with $10,000. He had seen the law clerk of the judge and tried to buy him off, but this was one straight town, not for sale. The judge was very concerned with public reputation and definitely not likely to let the biggest news story since the Tijuana road loose. Ernesto Duran had spoken at length to Andrew and Ted about a lawyer in La Paz. American lawyers were unable to practice here, so William was going to collaborate with a Mr. Gonzales—the only one of the four lawyers in La Paz who was not an alcoholic or too old to practice. We would see him tomorrow. William said, "The major thing to remember is that you all know nothing. There is no court or jury system here. There is one federal judge. He alone decides your innocence or guilt and subsequently your sentence. He has one year after the trial to sentence you unless the case warrants appeals court in Hermosillo. You are guilty until proven innocent. The trial must take place within seventy-two hours of the interrogation. This time for you three is up tomorrow morning. The charges against all three of you are the same. Acquisition, transportation, importation, and possession of 250 kilos of hashish. The maximum sentence is twenty-seven years." (I became feverish and Ted turned a little greener.) "However, there is no reason to believe he will hold Ted and Susan after tomorrow." (Jesus, Andrew, you have to bear it all.) "If, however, the verdict is guilty, then Gonzales and I will have to work out a defense and put in a plea for a new trial. Today, just relax. I am going to go out and buy you all the things you need, and bring back a good dinner from a restaurant. Susan, do you have a dress to wear to court?" "A dress?" I had to pause for a moment to remember that reality. "No. I ahhhhh no, I don't." William wanted to go out and buy one, but he didn't really have the time and I couldn't very well get a dress without trying it on. The ol' double standard crept up. The judge already hated me for living with someone out of wedlock and being a so-called doper, and William thought one dress and my image would be covered.

Ernesto Duran was slinking around and Andrew called him over. Ernesto laughed after Andrew told him our supposed problem. He said I had nothing to worry about. "Chino will take care of it." Chino, as it turned out, was the tailor in residence. "I will get him." Tailor in residence? Then Andrew explained to me that the jail here was very different from ours in the states. The men had separate cells, or were four to a room. Their cells were locked from 6:00 P.M. to 6:00 A.M. and then they were unlocked onto the courtyard outside their cells, there they could play basketball all day, just hang out, work on abalone carvings, work with silver or gold. There was one inmate who made cakes and delivered them to the town, one did the laundry for all the prisoners, and Chino, who did all the tailoring for the prisoners, the officials, and the townsfolk. It was a very strange but wonderful trip.

Chino was escorted out from behind the courtyard doors. He was a fabulous character—half-Chinese and half-Mexican. He had his own sewing machine in jail, Ernesto told us, and was a trusty, like Duran. He made clothes for the ten *Federales* and the *comandante* of the jail—all of those men were always immaculately dressed. He also made clothes for the majors in the army, the judge, and the wealthier women and children in the town. He was personally escorted and driven to the houses. He was small, slight, and wiry, with definite "not to be trusted" vibes. He came out of the prison to the reception room with about ten swatches of material and a big grin. He casually took my measurements and Ernesto translated as Chino told me that the dress would have epaulets, gold buttons, and two pockets. The color I picked was bright pink, hot pink; this was just too much to handle, a dressmaker in jail, right out of Fu Manchu—another fuckin' movie. He would come to my cell tomorrow morning early for a fitting. Laughlin paid him and he was taken away—oh happy, happy day. Then good ol' Roger asked if I had a bra (shit no), and the three of them, Andrew included, decided that I should wear Band-Aids on my nipples so as not to entice the judge.

Our time together was almost up—I held on to Andrew, and he had tears in his eyes. We told Laughlin that we needed toilet paper, tooth paste, distilled water, pillows, a nightgown for me, the list was endless and I wondered why, if everyone was so sure that I would be out tomorrow, this was necessary. The warden came back, motioned to us that it was time to leave, 3:30, and William promised us good food that night and made sure that from now on Andrew and Ted would have the chef (Louis) send over my meals at the same time theirs were served. There was so much new input to handle. A jail, with chefs and *haute couture,* a warden who could be paid off in whiskey, a new dress, a rather suspicious lawyer and my life, where was it going? I tried to act cheerful for Andrew, who tried to act cheerful for me, who tried not to hate us for God, who knew all the answers anyway. I told Andrew that we could work out a system of sending notes back and forth with Ernesto—of whom he too was slightly distrustful. He told me to play the tape deck and not to cry. It was so casual being with him, I couldn't believe they were taking me away. "Oh, Andrew!" I screamed, and everyone turned around to look, Laughlin shaking his head. "I love you, please Andrew, don't let them get us." I was crying and was ushered away by the old guard who shook his head and tried to grab my ass—the low-life. But then, who was I to delineate values of low or high? Is a dope smuggler a criminal? I mean, if I smoked it, someone had to bring it in, didn't he? I knew that I wasn't a criminal—I really only wanted to get high and make a fast buck—what was I to learn from the bust? That I should be more careful: Or that dope is bad? Or that I had lived a life in a delusion of phony spiritualism and thought that I was divine and protected? Were my values real, could I rationalize smuggling and then feel that Nixon was corrupt? Does Karma mean that you can't get money for something you don't earn? Was this a giant test for me? Was I paying off dues from other lifetimes? Where were the heavies of my generation with all the answers?

As I entered the cell, several policemen were carrying Juanita—screaming—out of the cell. She was in labor. All of her things were gone. No more nightly dances and eerie songs. I was left alone with the rats and my questions.

May 27. I sat down on the sleeping bag, my body exhausted, my mind tired of facing all the questions that I had no answers for. Twenty-seven years is a long time to be incarcerated. I would be fifty-two years old when I got out, much too old to settle, to even think of having children, which was one of my primary concerns in life. I wanted to live my life peacefully, take care of my old man, write, and have children. I felt that my desires were so simple, my needs so few, and yet I had been greedy for more: more dope, more money, more running. I was a princess all right, the princess of weakness, the princess of almost-ers, those who almost make it, have to fake it, never stop to consider what the consequences will be. Finally, in this self-made prison where I had lived, looking under every magic mushroom for an easy answer, I had put myself in a position where there was almost nothing that I *could* do. The easy life had led to a hard reality and I had to learn to cope with life myself—princess of the rats and lice and loony-tuners who pounded against my cell wall. I was alone now in the woman's cell—it was strange, and I wondered how long until a prostitute would be thrown in to accompany me. Although, as the district prosecutor had told me, prostitution was not legal in La Paz, the Mexicans had a realistic view of prostitutes and their trade. Every Sunday all the prostitutes in town had to report to the prison doctor, to be examined. If they were clean, so to speak, it was three quick peeks and they were back on the street. If, however, the examining doctor found V.D., they were given one week to clean it up; then if they were examined and found still infectious, or didn't report back the next Sunday, they were thrown into jail for fifteen days or released on fifty-peso bail. At least, I thought to myself, they had bail, and an occasional pimp to pay it for them. We had no bail. Occasionally a prostitute would be jailed for drunkenness.

At first I thought that being in jail with a prostitute, not a killer or psychopath, might be an interesting experience. But on consideration, who wanted to break bread or share bathroom facilities, however crude, with a walking case of gonorrhea? I started getting nervous. I wished Juanita could have stayed in the cell, at least she slept all the time. But my thoughts were interrupted by a clanging at the door—the guard brought in an old man, about fifty-five or so, with no teeth or hair and only three fingers. He smiled licentiously, and I felt weak in the knees. He pulled in a bucket, mop, and bottle of Lysol, and started to clean the cell. Apparently my cleaning efforts had been reported to the *comandante* of the jail, and so as not to shame the immaculate standards of the Bajans, he wanted to show me that they were clean too. However, the mop was filthy and the water gray, the Lysol was not Lysol and smelled almost as bad as the bathroom. I let him clean. My biggest triumph was that while he was washing down the floors, I could stand outside with the guard and smell the blossoms of the little tree. It was so beautiful outside, very hot, yet I would choose the heat to the coolness of the cell floor. The old man finished, smiled again, and waited as if I should pay him. I saw him eying the Krishna band, with its delicate little plastic figures, and I gave him one, an old man dressed in blue, portrayed playing the lute. The cleaning man loved it, dropped it into his pocket, and sauntered off. I sat down on the bed and turned on my Joni Mitchell tape. ". . . I wish I had a river, I could skate away on . . . ," me too baby, me too. I started to write a note to Andrew about the Brotherhood of the Light and trying to maintain our heads without the phony spiritualism and without phony projection of ourselves into roles that L.A. people use so frequently. I thought about Jerusalem and the tomb of King David high on Mt. Zion, where I had first been introduced to Jewish mysticism. The intangible and even unreachable keep the ignorant pupil in place, because they offer him both the fear of the unknown and an inability to deal with the known. I had entirely missed the point, I had never tried to appreciate myself. I fingered the ancient Moroccan coin I was wearing around my neck and tried to write to Andrew that we had been full of shit, because you sure in hell can't help your brother if you can't help yourself.

Another interruption. I quickly finished the note to Andrew, folded it and waited as the six o'clock guard opened the cell and gave me my dinner from Andrew. I handed him the note and a few pesos from Laughlin, I prayed he understood, at least I knew that he understood money. I took my dinner. It was from an excellent restaurant, shrimp, salad, baked potato, garlic toast, and chocolate cake. I had no goddam fork, and used my fingers; the food tasted outrageously good. I was thinking about what to drink when a small boy passed outside my cell selling orange pop. I called him over and bought one. (They even let the vendors come back to my cell.) The sky was turning black, I was feeling chilly and lighting a candle when the rather handsome face of Adolfo, head of the *Federales,* appeared at my cell door smiling. Then I heard a huge commotion and saw that there were five other policemen with him. They were carrying a huge man. He was very fine-looking, finely sensitive. He was crying and Adolfo was holding his hand. They opened my cell and I understood that the poor man was mentally disturbed and was to be locked up with the other prisoners behind me. I looked at him—his eyes saw me and for a moment he stopped and said in perfect English, "My name is Jaime, I love you." Then they carried him— once again crying—to the section behind the door. In all the turmoil, and because Adolfo had special affection for me, I slipped in with them. The area consisted of about ten cells on the left side— very primitive—I saw Tony, the crazy, naked, with his Yankee cap on, playing with his foot and watching TV. Felix was giggling on a mattress in the next cell, and they were opening up the third cell for Jaime. The cells led to a courtyard with a fountain. The men were supposed to be able to exercise or sit in the sun in the courtyard. An immense wall encircled the entire area, well guarded by police to prevent escapes. Adolfo was talking gently to Jaime—he seemed very tender with him. He was trying to give him a pill. Jaime looked up and saw me, spoke briefly to Adolfo, then Adolfo gave me a sign and Jaime called me over. He said, "Susana, you, you give me my pills. Do not be afraid, I won't hurt you." I walked over to the cell, stepped in and took the pills from Adolfo. Then I put them in Jaime's mouth; he took a drink of water and swallowed them, then looked at me. Adolfo motioned me to leave, at which point Jaime started to scream and I ran into my cell. The man was obviously bright, educated, for he spoke English with a good accent. I felt very sad as the guards piled out of my cell; Adolfo locked the huge metal door that led to the men's section, tipped his hat to me, walked out of my cell, and locked me up.

I could feel despair coming out of nowhere. I had to do something. I picked up my recorder. It brought back memories in a flood. Seven years old, playing the scales; then the flute for ten years; hours of practice and duets with my sister Barbra, who played the violin, and my little sister Elizabeth (Little Bit), who played the piano, and Israel where I played Sabbath songs on Friday night and later on Andrew and I pounding out our music so furiously. I switched on Roberta Flack's tape on the deck and played to accompany her. The air was cool and I realized how pathetic my tune sounded. Roberta sang "Angelitos Negros." She sang it in Spanish and I turned up the volume to the loudest and blew my recorder in time with the song while tears streamed down my face. I felt the Spanish heat of the song and the desolation of the Mexican poor who so needed reaffirmation that heaven is indeed for everyone. I felt my lost love for Andrew, and I played in descant with Roberta's voice and the moon and my heart. I cried, and when it was done, the silence was enormous and my chest was heaving up and down and I heard Jaime and Tony and Felix clapping and crying and Jaime yelled, "Play, Susan, play 'Angelitos Negros,' play, play. I am not crazy—I am like a black angel, angel, angel, I am going to Guadalajara for treatment. I am a man, a man. . . ." He banged against the bars, a man, hurt and lost and humiliated. I rewound the tape and started again, and the recorder sounded strong in the stone walls

as it echoed, and at my cell door appeared Adolfo and two guards,
looking strangely at me, and I played more beautifully than I had
ever played before, not for them, but for Jaime, because I knew he
believed in me. Then it all became too much for me. I turned off
the tape deck, put down the recorder, and blew out the candles. All
of them left the cell door but Jaime cried all night and screamed for
me to play.

Sometimes he was coherent and told me that he had gone to the
university, was an engineer and skin diver. Sometimes he was Jesus
Christ and I didn't know what to believe. Around twelve o'clock I
went to the bathroom and rinsed out the clothes I had been soaking
since the night before. I turned on the bulb, and looked at the
hideousness of my cell and the huge bugs on the walls, at the slime
that seeped up from the floor and at my pathetic broom and cleaners
and I cried as I ran cold water in the goddam red bucket and waited
for it to fill, then poured it on myself, half-frozen. I had forgotten
the soap in the cell and had to run and wash my hair and rinse off to
look nice for the judge who would certainly free me since I would
have Band-Aids on my nipples and gold buttons on my dress, and
was obviously not guilty. And I looked at the wall and shrieked
because there was a hole which led directly to Tony's cell and there
he was, in his stupid Yankee hat, his eye glued to the hole. At that
point I didn't care; he laughed and I finished and wrapped the towel
around me and turned off the light before I left. However, I plugged
up the hole with toilet paper. I put on another T shirt and my flag
underpants. I was shivering and had hot flashes; I was getting sick. I
fell into the sleeping bag, zipped it up and fell asleep, only to be
awakened five hours later by Jaime screaming, four guards looking
at me, and Chino waiting to have a fitting on the dress. Can you
believe it—a fitting? Oh, yeah, man, I forgot. This is my big day in
court, everyone has a day in court, so the saying goes. I shivered out
of the sleeping bag and thanked God for the T shirt which was long
enough to cover my underpants. My hair was still damp, but soon I
would be sweltering hot. I took the pink rag from Chino, went into
the bathroom, and tried it on. It had a mandarin collar, epaulets,
and gold buttons. The material was very thick. I didn't care if it was

long or short, but Chino did. He called me out and said, "You like?" I said, "Yeah man, like Yves St. Laurent." He smiled and said, "St. Laurent, him good too." He left with the guard to give the dress its final touches and I sat down to await trial; I had nothing to do but put on a lively tape, electric Led Zeppelin—I paced up and down, up and down, then a guard appeared at my door with a mug of steaming coffee and eggs and bacon in a blue-and-white bowl. It was food from Andrew prepared by Louise, the cook. Laughlin had arranged for me to eat three times a day. When food was distributed, Andrew would fill my bowl with food and the guard would bring it over to my side. This time along with the food was a sack containing Kleenex, toilet paper, powder, Nivea lotion for my skin, a nightgown with a note, "Just in case," in case I wasn't released, I imagined. Also included was an alarm clock, more candles, incense, a copy of *Vogue,* a pillow and pillowcase, radio batteries, a box of chocolate cookies, a bag of apricots, a box of raisins, a new mug, my silverware, and tweezers—I knew they had had to bribe the warden for that—and other things. I thanked the guard, ate my breakfast thinking, at this rate I'll gain weight in jail, and put away my new possesions. Suddenly a guard appeared at my cell, shoved my dress in and made like, get dressed, lady. I ran to the bathroom and took two Band-aids with me. I tried to cover my nipples, but I was sweating so much it was impossible. Finally I got them on, put on my dress, pulled back my hair, and debated as to whether I should put make-up on. I felt rather strange making-up today, so I decided to go for the natural look. The guards came to get me as I was putting my sandals on. I grabbed my purse and the cross the young boy had given me; you never know.

Then I was marched to the office where Andrew and Ted were standing with William and a small Mexican man they identified as Mr. Gonzales, our Mexican attorney. He shushed us, and said in slow, halting English that he was sure that I would get out today, please not to worry. Then Laughlin, who spoke Spanish pretty well, translated as Gonzales went over the questions the judge would ask each one of us—we would be questioned separately. The first question Gonzales would ask me would be if I knew that the armoire had

had hash in it—this seemed like a pretty stupid way to start things. Why not ask about something like background, to build up my case or character? But there was no time to question him and I had to assume that someone, somewhere, I hoped my lawyer, knew what he was doing. Anyhow, no, I never knew what the armoire had contained. No, I never opened it. Yes, I was living with Andrew. I was twenty-five, not twenty-nine. And that's it. At the end I was supposed to talk about my innocence. This seemed a shitty defense, even by my uninformed standards. Laughlin reassured me that he would be in the room with me and not to worry. Ted gave me the peace sign, I mean really. Andrew just tried to give me strength, which was hard, because he was shaking. After the trial the judge had twenty-four hours before pronouncing decision. Laughlin would stay until the verdict came in and later that day I would see Andrew and Ted again. I wished everyone well, and was escorted back to my cell again, where I waited, in the dress, for three hours, until I was called. Everything in Mexico happens so slowly that a three-hour wait is nothing. I was so nervous that I fell asleep sitting up. The guard came to get me and I was escorted out by three *Federales* with machine guns who kept whistling at me.

The ride to the courthouse was nerve-wracking—to say the very least. I was beginning to feel nauseous. I couldn't smoke. The car pulled up in front of the courthouse and I screamed at Andrew—who was handcuffed and had his old straw hat on—being escorted back to jail with a ten-man police escort, as if he were a killer. Laughlin had a Nikon camera and was talking and taking photographs like mad; he smiled reassuringly. I was led into a dilapidated old room with a single fan that did no good. There was the fat woman I recognized from the interrogation. Laughlin slipped in and told me that the judge was in the other room with the district prosecutor and his clerk; all had gone well. I saw Adolfo in the corner combing his hair, he smiled, showed all his pearly whites and trying to reassure me. But I knew that he would have no influence on the verdict.

Mr. Gonzales emerged from the small room that contained the judge's chambers. He smiled at me too, came over, and said not to worry. He had talked to the judge and everything was all right. Laughlin sat down on my left and told me that he had been with both Andrew and Ted for their trials and that the judge had seemed very understanding. They had the least amount of evidence on Ted, he was merely a friend who had stopped in to visit us on his way to Guadalajara (so they thought!). Of course, both Laughlin and I knew the truth. I resented Ted, he was the so-called brains, which meant only that he was smart enough to cover his ass. Andrew was the one who was really in trouble. As far as I was concerned, the judge would maybe find it hard to believe that I was living with Andrew and knew nothing of the drug deal. But Laughlin assured me that the judge was an old man and could be swayed easily.

I was already starting to have my doubts about both Laughlin and Gonzales. I thought that an older man like the judge would be set in his ways and more likely to be offended that Andrew and I had been living together. The D.P. came out of the judge's chambers. "Hello Susan, how are you today?" (Oh, great, man, I feel like I'm going to a party.) "And how does it feel, Susan, to have all of your things in your cell with you?" (Just like the Hilton, man, just like the Hilton, why don't you come over for lunch today? We're having spider scampi.) Laughlin and Gonzales got up and Laughlin took my arm and escorted me into the judge's chambers. I took one look at the judge, in that sweaty little box they called his office and I figured, pass on this one, Susan.

I later took to calling him El Pinche Juez, or the Bastard Judge, almost untranslatable into English. He was about five-one, with a short-sleeved, filthy gray shirt on, and egg in his mustache, and around sixty-eight or seventy. This was it, folks, the only representative of the Mexican Federal Judiciary system in La Paz, Baja California sur Mexico. He moved so slowly that I figured he was senile, and my life rested in his shaky hands. He smiled at me, however, everyone there smiled, and I sat in front of his desk with Gonzales beside me and Laughlin in the back of the room (about three feet away); he had received special permission to be there. The judge read his notes for about fifteen minutes and swatted away the flies, can you dig it? My own trial and the judge couldn't speak English.

The questioning then began. I was never sworn in, the judge's assistant, whom Laughlin had approached the night before to see if the judge could be bribed, sat behind the judge and took notes in shorthand. The questions were exactly as Gonzales had said. The judge would ask the questions, Gonzales would translate. As I answered the questions the judge's eyes would drop to breast level. Hey, this girl's innocent, she wears Band-Aids on her nipples. Finally my time came to talk about my innocence. I stated that I had never known that Andrew was receiving drugs; that we did not live that type of existence (at least not since we had been busted); that I was an educated and responsible woman from a fine family, and that I thought the whole thing was a mistake.

The judge thanked me, picked up a book, and started reading. That was the sign that court was adjourned. I left with Laughlin, Gonzales, and two *Federales*. Before I left, I asked to go to the bathroom and was escorted through a courtyard overgrown with flowers and ferns. Hidden in the undergrowth were small chairs and some statues. It was really a lovely little courtyard, and I wanted to sit down, but knew that that was an impossibility. Directly in front of the bathroom stood the armoire, tall, majestic, and full of shit: I could even smell the pungent odor of the hash—it was still there. I went to the bathroom, came out, and got into the car. On the drive back Laughlin got out his camera and talked to me. He told me we would all meet tomorrow morning and hear the verdict. He gave me $100 in pesos for expenses and told me that dinner would be sent in again. He told me that I had done very well in court and that he was taking pictures of the jail in case we ever had to make a fast escape. Arriving, he walked with me back to my cell, snapping pictures as we went, kissed me on the cheek, slipped me a valium, and left. I never saw him again.

It was about 6:30 when I finally changed my clothes, washed in water I had saved from the night before, and got into my Levis and T shirt. I was sitting on the cot, listening to the radio, amazed at all the goddam commercials. They were all spoken so quickly that I found it hard to believe that even the Mexicans understood them. The commercials were all very jovial, and happy female voices sang about soup and toilet paper. Mexican music, however, was a different story. It was very earthy, romantic, and heavy-atmosphere music. Mexican music, much like Country and Western, deals with the basic questions of the simple life: love, infidelity, death—in that order. All the crazies behind me, Tony, Felix, and later others sang along with the music and cried at the sad parts. Jaime started to scream for me. He yelled out that he spoke French and German and English and Italian. He told me he had been a spy for the Mexicans in the Second World War, I didn't even know that they had been in it. He yelled about how they had locked him up like an animal, and then he spoke to me about philosophy and Kant, his famous friend, and how Jaime felt that Kant was the only purist of all the philosophers. And I sat on the floor beside the metal door and talked back to him about my beliefs about God, and how we have all been here before and how we are all connected. We laughed, and then he cried and asked me to forgive him and not think less of him as a man because he cried.

The cell door jingled open and my fine dinner of clams and rice and ice cream was brought in by Adolfo and Jaime's brother. They had come to bring Jaime his food and chocolate and pills. When they opened the door Jaime screamed for me and his brother apologized. I said that it was nothing. He told me in broken English that Jaime was really a good boy, sick in the head, very smart, going to a clinic for the shock treatment. He was schizophrenic and when these periods came over him he would drink and not take his medicine; without his medicine he could not function as a single person but had delusions of grandeur and thought that he was a number of poeple. I walked over to Jaime's cell where he lay in his underpants on the floor, crying. He spit at me, he told me to go fuck myself—he was sane, I was crazy. Then he told me that he loved me, and I gave him his medicine. He apologized to me and I took off the Moroccan coin that I was wearing around my neck and put it around his neck. We both cried, Adolfo looked away, and Jaime's brother tried to give me money. I walked into my cell and tried to eat, but I couldn't. Adolfo and Jaime's brother left with the police who were all talking about me. I recognized one from the previous day's drilling. He smiled. I took a valium and got into the sleeping bag. It was 8 o'clock but I fell asleep, exhausted.

At three o'clock in the morning I was awakened by a lot of commotion outside my cell door. A huge guard turned on the naked bulb and threw a young woman on the floor. She was small and dark and dressed in a short, sleazy, red dress. She was also drunk and belligerent as hell. She threw up on the floor and then saw me. She grabbed me and started to kick me and pull my hair—then threw me onto the floor. The cell stank of liquor and vomit: my first introduction to a prostitute. I spent a cold and frightened night on the floor. The guards got us up at six o'clock. Jaime was screaming for my help, he was afraid. The prostitute slept on and on. My fifth day in jail had begun.

*D*ay fifth of the jail riff. Now I sit in my cell and have a smoke, laugh at this part of the continuing joke. The guards had left the cell, Jaime continued to scream and I was sick from the smell. I watched the little prostitute snoring on the bed. She could not have been any older than twenty-four or twenty-five, yet she had fought with the ferocity of a caged animal and had hard lines around her mouth like those of a fifty-year-old neurotic. The guards had all nudged one another when they saw her on the bed, "Ah, Juanita." "Hee hee, Juana." So I gathered that her name was Juanita, the same as the mentally retarded, pregnant Juanita who had probably had her child by now. She had been vicious with me in the night, but things always look different in the morning. I felt sorry for her; there was vomit in her hair and on her dress. There was a clanking on the cell door, a guard with a steaming mug of coffee and some eggs in the blue-and-white bowl for me. I drank the coffee, but was too nauseous to eat the eggs. The old cleaning man entered the cell again and pushed Juanita with his broom. She woke up with a start, snarled, and looked around, then shook her head, got directly up, and went to the bathroom. She had been here before. I rolled up my sleeping bag and stepped outside to wait under my little tree while the man cleaned my cell. I wondered if Juanita would steal my things. I wouldn't guard my possessions too carefully, but didn't want to share my things with her. I was standing under the tree, basking in the sunlight, when I saw the young mechanic approach. He had missed two days, but had now returned to see me. I wondered if the guard would hassle him, but apparently they were old friends; they kissed each other on the cheeks. The mechanic asked a few questions about Susanita, and pulled out an orange, a box of cigarettes, and a candy bar for me. I didn't know what I could ever give him to thank him. He shook my hand and said, "Tommy, Tommy," several times, and I said, *"Gracias amigo Tommy, gracias."* This was as far as my limited Spanish permitted, but it was enough. He laughed at the sun and his eyes were clear and bright. *"Amiga, Susana amiga."*

The old man exited from the cell, his cleaning done, and I entered. Sitting on the floor was Juanita looking like a wet red dishrag. She had washed—in all of her clothes. She looked up sheepishly at me, afraid me, nervous me, not-able-to-maintain-my calm me, opened her hands to take in the cell, and made a gesture like vomiting. She said, "Sorry, sorry, sorry." "Sorry" sounded Chinese the way she said it. I didn't know what to say, since my vocabulary was so limited, so I gave her my eggs and tortillas, and she ate greedily with her hands. I wanted to talk to her and ask her about her life, what was the goddam word in Spanish for "life"? She wiped her hands on her dress, climbed up on the smelly mattress, and fell back to sleep again, her mouth open, snoring. I had to have something to do to keep my mind off the craziness at hand, and to avoid worry about the verdict, which I was to get from Laughlin this morning. I tried to read *Narcissus and Goldmund* again. I became absorbed in Goldmund's flights of emotion and didn't notice the guard at my cell door. An hour had passed. The guard opened the door, motioned me to follow him, and I grabbed my purse. Then I was out in the air: run, walk, play, May is nearly gone, is it June yet? I thought of Andrew and my sentence as I walked to the offices of the jail and the room I called the sitting room. It was cold and empty today. As I was walking in I saw Adolfo and four *Federales* flanking a small, heavy man with two .38s slung on his hips and clean gray pants. It was the man who had checked my arms for needle marks, which were now gone except for the large bump near my wrist where I had missed the vein, tied the tie too tightly, and collected the dope in my skin. This man standing in front of me was one of the last vestiges of the Wild West, packin' his guns and giving orders. He tipped his goddam sombrero and I wondered silently why that sign was an indication of respect for a woman. The doors that were normally shut, leading to the permanent prison for the men, were open, behind them a door of bars. I saw that the men were passing out mail to the prisoners, who had gathered around the barred door. They were a motley crew, most of them tan from exposure to the sun in the courtyard; many wore long hair and cut-offs. Andrew and Ted were being let out of there. When had they been transferred to the permanent-prisoner section and taken out of the transient quarters? It was appalling to me that they were no longer considered temporary prisoners.

Andrew ran up and grabbed me around the waist, Ted gave me a loving hello and the peace sign—the goddam peace sign again, like a fuckin' hippy. He was greener than ever and looked like he had lost ten pounds. Ernesto Duran entered from another door and the four of us sat down. My first question, after all the hellos and how-are-yous were out, was, where was Laughlin? Ted cleared his throat and told me that the *comandante* had gotten very suspicious of his picture-taking; in fact, he had ordered him out of Baja, never again to return. They were afraid that Laughlin was the head of a big-time operation. Ted liked this, it inflated his ego, the asshole. If he knew how ridiculous he looked in his nervous condition, he'd forget about big-time anything. Anyhow, they were afraid that Laughlin was from the Mafia and was going to plan our escape; not too stupid, these folk. Good-by Laughlin. Andrew kissed me and said, "Honey, baby, in fact they are so nervous about our escaping that they're calling in the army to watch the jail every night. Can you believe it, the Baja extension of the Mexican Army is going to waste soldiers on the Edificio M. Sobarzo. What's the matter, honey, don't you see how funny it is?" Yeah, oh sure, the whole thing was unbelievably humorous, me in jail and weird lawyers taking pictures and the army coming to guard me. I was crying because I knew the answer to my next question. "Andrew, the judge found us guilty, didn't he? We got twenty-seven years, didn't we? We're going to fuckin'

rot in jail, choke on tortillas and false hopes. Oh, Andrew, I'm
sorry, I know it's not your fault. I just can't believe it, all our talk
about love and God and karma and vibes and we got caught at some
stupid plot to make a lot of money." Andrew shook his head and the
rock of Gibraltar, Ted, chicken, snipe, sneak, started to cry too. Ernesto spoke, "Listen, Susan, yes, you did get caught, and found
guilty. But you are in the hands of a very competent attorney, Mr.
Gonzales. None of your American attorneys are going to be able to
practice here, your money can't buy you out, you must get into the
Mexican way of waiting with patience. Do you know how I got
here? I came to visit some friends in jail and smuggled two joints to
them in a loaf of bread, the police found them. I got five years, but
due to good behavior, and the fact that I was useful to them, my
sentence was commuted to two years and I am a trusty. (That's fabulous, Ernesto, maybe I'll get my sentence commuted to fifteen years
and can become a trusty like you.) "Anyhow, Susan, Laughlin told
me a few things to tell you." Ted aside: "Don't worry, baby, we got
connections." (I thought, yeah, I know all about your connections.)
"Laughlin is a heavy, we'll all be out soon." Then back to Ernesto:
"Susan, there was a box of pills found in Ted's suitcase, the judge
had a chemist burn it and from this test he considers that a chemical
analysis of the pills was done. The snuffer said that the pills smelled
like hash, and that is enough for the judge. They are claiming that
the pills are yours, 150 tabs of hash." At this point I was absolutely
amazed. Hash is not compressible into tabs, and what kind of test
was that? To burn the tabs in a laboratory! "But Ernesto, those tabs
weren't hash, they're Innerclean herbal laxatives, and they weren't
mine. Mine were in the medicine cabinet, probably still are. Those
are Ted's. Ted, tell them they were yours, for Christ's sake! Get
goddam Gonzales to take more tests, they're laxatives for God's
sake, they *make* you shit, they *aren't* shit." Ted sheepisly shook his
head "It wouldn't make any difference if I claimed the pills were
mine or not Susan, they'll see soon that they aren't hash." Oh God,
not me, this shouldn't be me, twenty-seven years for someone else's
laxatives.

Ernesto and Ted started to talk up the merits of Gonzales and

Andrew and I began to talk softly to each other. I looked at my man, he looked at me, and we both knew that we'd never really be able to talk the same way as before, when we had pretended we were so high. He told me how much he loved me and that he would take the whole blame if he knew that in doing so I would get out. "Honey, we've paid off the warden, Ted and I got a cell together. It's amazing over on our side; the guys all have their cells fixed up, sometimes four men to a room with bunk beds. And I'm making a mobile for the wall. We play basketball all day, and listen to the tapes and play the guitars. The cook told me he'll make sure you get good food, just wash your bowl out in distilled water after every meal and send it back with the guard. There's some kind of arrangement on Thursdays and Sundays when the women can visit their men all day, from nine o'clock in the morning until six. We're trying to get to talk to the *comandante* to arrange it for me and you. It's like a family picnic, honey, honey, listen to me. We can cook and make love in a friend's single cell and get high. Yeah, some friends somehow get the dope in. I know your conditions are bad, but Laughlin got all he could for you, and we have money. Your people will probably send you money, you get the equivalent of two pesos a day from the government when you're in jail. They pay you. I love you, baby, I know how hard this is for you, just try to maintain, that's the name of the game."

I listened to Andrew and grew distant and I said, "Yeah, I would be thrilled to come to your apartment and see your stamp collection. We could make beautiful music together." I would accept the date for a week from Sunday. I told him that I felt sick, he reminded me not to drink the water, and I told him about Jaime and the prostitute. He said he would arrange to pay her bail so I would have the cell alone again. He was, however, highly suspicious of Jaime, conferred with the mental giant Ted, and decided I should keep away. I never listened to him about that. I guess I never really listened to Andrew again. Once you lose respect for a man, whether it was your fault in part or not, you start to look at him in a new way; I saw him as helpless. We were startled out of our little *tête-à-tête* by Ernesto. "Susan, it seems as though your parents have arrived in town.

They called this morning and will call back later. Apparently they are waiting for some friend from Mexico City to meet them here. I talked to them. Your mother sounded hysterical. But she did tell me how anxious they were to get you out." I felt like someone had hit me over the head, like my whole world had caved in. My parents, my wealthy parents who had gently gone through life in their fairy-tale castle of fine art and fine antiques, where we children had performed for them with dance classes, music lessons, and good grades. We went to beach cottages in Massachusetts in the summer and my mother took sculpting lessons. They didn't know anything about American prisons, wait until they caught my act in the Baja beauty spa. The guilt was getting me. Andrew, who knew my family history, he says to me, "Sister, if they hassle you, tell them to fuck off, see, 'cause we'll get you out." Yeah Andrew, just like you got me in. What was I now in their eyes, a criminal? How was I going to face them?

I didn't have time to articulate to Andrew how I felt; our time together for the day was over. Before they left, Andrew gave me a Spanish-English dictionary so I could try to communicate with the guards. We kissed good-by. Ernesto Duran told me to act strong, Ted gave me the peace sign, this time I gave him the finger. I watched them being locked up again and was on my way to my cell, when Duran flew up, grabbed my hand, and told me that my mother was on the phone. I broke out in a sweat. Slowly, very slowly, I edged back to the phone and lit my first cigarette in two days. Ernesto watched me carefully. "You can handle it girlie." "Hello mother." Silence. "How do you like La Paz? I really am sorry I put you and Daddy to such trouble. When are you coming over?" And with this I broke down and started to cry. Now she knew she had me, I needed her now. "Susan, don't cry. We're here. And don't ask me questions like do I like La Paz. We're here to help you, even though you don't deserve it." (That was true enough.) "We won't come today to see you. We've been flying for fifteen hours. We had to fly from Pittsburgh to Chicago, lay over there for four hours, and then to L.A. That took nine hours altogether and you know how long it takes to get to this hell-hole. We're meeting a friend of your father's, a businessman, very influential. He will be here later and come to the jail with us in the morning to help us translate. We brought you things. We don't know that much of what is going on but we did find out from Ernesto Duran that your maximum sentence is for twenty-seven years. Who is he? You are not to talk to Andrew. Do you understand that?" (Oh mother, please.) "We're staying at Las Brisas Hotel if you need us. We love you and we'll see you tomorrow." "Good-by mother." Good-by fairy-tale mother, this is the real nitty gritty.

I put the phone down and sat, exhausted. Ernesto told me to take it easy and I was escorted back to my cell. I saw Juanita on the floor, she pointed to the bed. She wanted me to know that I could sleep on the mangy cot. I put my sleeping bag on the cot and watched the sunset behind my tree. So this is how it all ends, so ugly. Me and a hooker and my family. Oh shit, what was the point?

And the sun set. It was beautiful, as usual. The guards arrived in front of the cell and started to drill, as usual. They laughed so loud that I thought they were doing it to upset me. So I turned my tape deck on as loudly as possible and put Led Zeppelin on. It was so loud that I even jumped; it created pandemonium for the drillers who couldn't even hear the sergeant. He, a very cold and hard man, came over to my cell door, pulled out a knife (I must have turned green with that big shot trying to scare me); then snorted. But I still refused to turn down the music, a last vestige of my pointless rebellion. He pulled a lever on the wall outside and the electricity went off. He got the last laugh.

I waited until the drill was over, and he came back and turned the power on. The four guards came in to check the men behind me. I walked in behind them to give Jaime his medicine. He was very pale and quiet and never said a word to me. When I was leaving he gave me a note. It said: *Thank you for being a kind woman. Will you marry me?* I shook my head as I walked away. The guard brought me dinner, beans, pork, rice, salad, and two tortillas. Juanita eyed my food and slithered up to the guard. He looked directly into my eyes and grabbed her breast; he played with it for a while, then sauntered off and brought her back some food from a small stand across the street. A little sex, a little food. By now it was dark, and I played the recorder for Jaime. He cried out for the music of Bach and Beethoven, and I tried to remember some simple Bach. But he fell out early, maybe in a catatonic state. I was left with Juanita. She smiled at me and sat beside me on the bed. I got out my dictionary. She kept touching my face and repeating the word *"bonita,"* which means "pretty." I asked her, in I'm sure very peculiar Spanish, about her life. She never answered. Communication came to a standstill. Then the same guard returned and Juanita went over to the bars, where they talked. I went into the bathroom and decided to shower—or bucket, as I had come to call it. I got undressed and threw buckets of cold water over my head. I hummed some Spanish music and washed my hair. I was just drying off when Juanita and the guard walked in. What in God's name? She motioned me to follow them and they pointed to the bed. The guard kept looking behind him, the cell door was shut. She pointed to the bed and took my hand and the hand of the guard, Alberto. Like let's get it on, man. Jesus Christ, I had never even been into anything like that with anyone, ever, let alone a drunk Mexican prostitute with venereal disease and a jail guard. But how could I defend myself? I started to scream like I had never screamed before, I yelled for God and my father, but especially for the *comandante* of the jail. The minute I yelled for the *comandante,* the guard ran out of the cell and started to wring his hands, *"Susanita, no problema,* shh-shhh." Like shit, you lowdown man, get a girl at her worst. Soon Adolfo appeared at the cell door, my hero. Jesus, it was like being attacked by a lion and having a leopard appear to help you. I couldn't explain myself. He kept shaking his head and saying, *"Miedo, miedo."* I looked it up in my new dictionary, it meant "fear." I said, *"Sí."* By now, Jaime was up and screaming, "My love, my love. I'll help you!" I just tuned everything out. Adolfo left, never knowing what had gone on. Who could I talk to that would understand me? I wrote a note to Andrew explaining what was happening. He would tell the warden, who would tell the *comandante,* who didn't care. I was shaking, terrified and nauseous. Juanita was scared and slept on the floor. I scoured my purse for a pill so that I could sleep, and found nothing. I began to wonder if I would ever get out of jail, karma sharma, it would depend upon my parents, and then what? Me with them and their reality that I had rejected years ago; could they afford to keep me in the style which I had rejected?

Tonight there is only dampness and despair. The terror of being alone. The pain of being with a soul I cannot like.

I got into the sweaty sleeping bag and fell into a sweaty sleep. *Buenos noches,* cock-a-roaches, and you fucking crickets too!

I slept unsoundly for five hours and was awakened by the four guards who came to open up the cells behind me and check things out. It was six o'clock in the morning, my sixth day in jail, and my parents would be here soon. I wanted to go back to sleep, but it was already hot and I was sweaty. I walked into the bathroom and looked at my face in the mirror Laughlin had brought me. I had a yellowish cast over my deep tan, and looked like shit. I threw some water in my face. I was getting acclimated to my surroundings; this was natural for me because I normally had no trouble adjusting to new things, but getting accustomed to jail is frightening—you get into the rut of being locked up. It is like returning to the womb which is safe and warm. What then becomes frightening is the outside world where problems that are unavoidable become far away; it seems safer to stay in jail. I noticed this later in the faces of many of the prisoners, who seemed content and almost stoned. Still looking at myself in the mirror, I felt someone looking at me, and I noticed that the wad of toilet paper I had shoved into the hole in the wall was on the floor. Tony must be glued to the hole; I went over, and instead of his eye peering back at me I was confronted with his lips. He spoke very softly and told me he wanted some cigarettes. I slipped about ten through the hole. Lately I had been smoking less and enjoying it less. Juanita was sleeping on the floor, snoring again. I sat on my bed edge and waited, it was like waiting for Godot, my fate, or my answer; I guess I was waiting for someone to rescue me. Tommy appeared at the cell door, smiling and bearing gifts, as usual. This time he gave me St. Francis's prayer in Spanish, forever locked inside its plastic covering, a chocolate bar, and some fresh dates. He never failed, always bringing me gifts in variety and never accepting a thing from me. I saw his young guard friend approaching behind him; he put his finger up to his mouth, including me in on the joke and the secret. The guards always tried to cheer me up and slapstick comedy was a basic form of their humor. He crept up slowly and silently, got behind Tommy, and yelled quite loudly. Tommy jumped up in the air, made tracks to leave, and when he saw that it was his friend, wrestled him to the floor: the Abbott and Costello of the penal system. I laughed and clapped my hands gleefully to thank them for their efforts. The guard opened up my cell door and handed me a steaming mug of coffee *con leche,* and a bowl of eggs, potatoes, bacon, and raisin toast. How good this food had come to taste to me! There was also a thermos of freshly squeezed orange juice. Andrew liked to send me things, it gave him something to do. I opened the thermos and found a note from him. (This thermos became one of our primary ways of smuggling very personal notes.) The note said that the *comandante* had told him that I was to have permission to visit him on Thursdays and Sundays, like the wives and families of the other prisoners. The *comandante* had also said that we could send notes to each other and see each other briefly during the week; in fact, we were to get together that morning. He also wrote that Ted had arranged to pay the bail of Juanita the next day.

I felt considerably happier and thanked the guard for the food and note. I thought at this time that he was our friend and that he risked his job to smuggle notes to us. I later found out that all the guards brought everything to the *comandante,* including the thermos, and he had Ernesto Duran translate our notes for him. Sometimes he didn't have time and the notes sat on his desk unread and finally he would send them over. But not one of the guards would risk his neck for either me or Andrew, not until much later. I washed my dishes and put on a pair of pink jeans and a clean top. It is very difficult to maintain one's feelings of femininity in prison; but I tried hard.

I put Jackson Brown's tape on the deck and danced around the cell until the old cleaning man came. This time I stayed in the cell with him and showed him the Lysol I had, the clean mop, the toilet-paper rack that I had made out of old wood, and the incense I lit for the odors. He was especially interested in the incense. He laughed at me while I danced, but as he was leaving he called the guard over and they conferred on some point about me. They kept repeating the same thing over and over again and pointing at my face. Thank God for the ol' *diccionario.* The word they kept repeating was yellow; apparently I looked quite yellow and unhealthy to them. As they were leaving another guard came waltzing over and indicated that I was to come too. I didn't know if it was to see Andrew or my parents. I took my purse, turned off the tape, and prayed it wasn't my parents yet. I wasn't quite ready.

As it turned out, Andrew was in the reception room of the jail looking very calm and the best I had seen him look for a long time. He stood up and took me in his arms and the guards walked away. "Baby, I got special permission from the *comandante* to see you today, alone. Ted is writing Loretta a letter." (Loretta was Ted's wife.) "Firstly, I want you to know that I have all the faith in the world that we'll be released soon. If not me, then you. Ernesto assures me that Gonzales is a good man." (However, I personally wondered about Duran.) "Listen, honey, in all the turmoil I somehow managed to let slip to Duran that you had been busted before, but that you have no record. Now before you start on me . . ."

Infuriated, scared, and nervous, I said, "You asshole, why did you think you could trust him?"

"Susan, I apologize, a mistake, but anyhow, he told me it's not valid evidence in a Mexican court, so don't worry about that."

Then I told him about Juanita and the guard and he became furious. We were to see the *comandante* in a few minutes, he had requested it, so until then we just sat there and held hands and thought of better days. Adolfo came out of the *comandante*'s office and motioned us in. We walked in holding hands. There was the arrogant little *comandante* sitting at his desk. The only wall decorations were guns, the guns of the ten *Federales* who worked under him: machine guns, rifles, and pistols. Nice décor. The *comandante* looked up and said, "Susan." He spoke English fairly well, so Andrew had told me. "Susan, you must be careful. If you want to see Andrew Thursdays and Sundays you must follow the rules. Your cell is your house, not like that of your parents, but I will have a sink put in for you. Do not try to escape, army come tonight." Then he pulled out a long note that I had written to Andrew, and I realized with a start that he could confiscate all of our notes, he was the head of the jail, and the guards would show him everything. "What means this, Susan, honey? Honey, it is for food?" What could I say? He started to laugh at me, then he saw my rather hurt and slightly angry expression; I hated anyone to laugh at me. I said, "Stop laughing." He stopped and looked up and as gently as Adolfo had spoken to Jaime he said, "Do not ever be afraid of me." He said it in such a way that I knew how afraid of him all the *Federales* were, and I knew how all the police were terrified of him, and I realized that no one ever treated him like a man or talked to him like a person and even though I was a prisoner, he wanted my friendship.

Andrew proceeded in fairly good Spanish to tell the *comandante* about the guard's attempts, with the aid of Juanita, to get me into a sex caper. The *comandante* became furious and sent Adolfo, his right-hand man, to gather all the guards together. The order was to leave me alone, or face him, something few of them wanted to do. His temper unleashed was wild. I decided to try for a long shot. Right before we left I said, *"Señor comandante,* with great respect, if it would be possible, on one Thursday or Sunday, to give a music concert for the prisoners. Andrew would play the guitar and I would play the recorder, and together we would sing. We would make no trouble. "For a minute I thought the *comandante* was going to laugh, then he said, "Your music, Susana, I know. I listen to your 'Angelitos Negros' when you play for Jaime. Concert is good idea. Better if you play Bach or Beethoven." (I was astonished, another revelation that I indeed had some class snobbery.) "But I'm afraid Susana

make the men too wild." "Too wild? I would be with Andrew playing." "All right, enough, we shall see. Andrew goes back to his cell
now, you will stay out there. Your parents come."

I thanked the man for his time, but was really too nervous about
seeing my parents to react normally. Andrew commented to me
when they were escorting us out what a strange man the *comandante*
was, full of incongruities. He had listened in when I had played for
Jaime, and had liked it. And he preferred Bach and Beethoven.
Many of the Mexicans were so puzzling to me. They seemed so har-
dened on the outside, yet the old adage was true: the way to insult a
Mexican was to comment on his mother. The Mexican respect for
the family was very high. I found this respect much akin to the Jewish ideology concerning the family. The Mexicans were so impressed
with my parents, and with the idea that my parents believed in my
innocence, that they treated me like a better person than they had
when I was first brought into the prison. Andrew's family could
never afford the trip down, and Ted's wife was a little too bizarre-
looking for their respect. It was the family unit as a whole that
really impressed them. Somehow a family that believed in you,
especially if you were a foreigner, made you seem less a criminal.

The guards were pulling Andrew away, he looked at me, I looked
at him, and he sent a part of himself to me. I sent a little of myself
back. Andrew knew, he said so softly as they locked him up, "I'm
right with you honey, your parents can't take you away. . . ." But
I knew how vulnerable I would be. I walked over to a bench and sat
down, the guards' eyes never leaving me. My parents would find a
disenchanted me, wanting to be free. And when you are disenchanted with your life, you have no defense. What could I possibly
say to them about values and their middle-class bourgeois way of
life, when I was in jail for smuggling dope? You can't get something for nothing; my father had always told me that. You only get
what you earn. According to them, I was getting my just deserts,
although I knew deep in my heart that I was not meant to live in
jail. I felt so far away from Andrew and yet I loved him still. He
was my only reality there, and yet I knew we would never share the
same reality again. I didn't feel that I was deserting him, I didn't

know then what I know now, whatever that may be. And then at that moment I turned around and saw my mother and father and a strange man talking to one of the guards. My God, the culture shock! From methedrine madness to a family reunion. The last time I had seen them was December 1971; then I had gone to Los Angeles for a party, telling them that I would see them in a few days. Now it was the end of May in 1972.

My mother saw me first. She walked over, chic as always, in the heat or rain or snow, in white pants and top and sandals. But she never took off her sun glasses; her eyes were too swollen from crying. I felt such guilt that I couldn't respond with love, such self-hate that I came off as being distant. She was sobbing; now it was my turn to comfort her, and I stood up and saw my father in a suit, an expensive tie, his gentle eyes and truthful mouth, his handsomeness showing through, yet he looked much shorter than I had remembered him. We looked at each other and my eyes begged, "Don't judge me too harshly." His gaze penetrated mine and I lowered my eyes. Times had changed. Susan, their darling, their piece of brown velvet. Could she no longer manipulate them with her beauty and vitality? My mother cried, I held her, she whispered, "Why, Susan, why? Was it the money? We don't know if we can get you out. This man is a friend of your father's, his name is Manuel, he flew in from Mexico City to see Gonzales and help us." And then more tears, but finally more sharply, "You look so defiant, Susan, you little whore . . ." And I hated her for the name-calling and wanted to leave and then my father walked up, no kisses. "Susan, hello. I'd like you to meet Mr. Cervantes." No emotion, like he was reading about it in *The New York Times*. Then me, "How do you do, Mr. Cervantes." What next? I couldn't say "How nice that you're trying to get me out of jail."

Whatever I was thinking or planning couldn't have turned out worse than what actually happened. The doors to the men's section opened up and Gonzales came out with Andrew and Ted. He had apparently come to see them when Andrew and I were with the *comandante,* and he had stayed with Ted until Andrew came back. Andrew had on cut-offs and I looked at him with the eyes of my

mother. He certainly didn't look like an Ivy Leaguer, but then neither did I. He came over and walked up to my mother, and this
refined lady, she started to glare at him like he never, ever could
have been with her daughter. He looked at me, thinking he had the
whole scene covered, and winked, said, "See you later, honey." By
now my father was shaking his head, and the guards took Andrew
away. Gonzales walked over to introduce himself to Mr. Cervantes
and my father. Ted waved, he was being billed as the innocent one.
My mother, picking right up on the phony vibes, said, "He looks so
sad. That Andrew sure knows how to get his friends in trouble."
She wouldn't know until much later that Ted was the originator of
the deal and that Andrew saved Ted's ass by never, ever copping to
the truth. Gonzales was gone; my father and the spiffily dressed Cervantes had sent him to get photostat copies of my interrogation and
the minutes of the trial. We all sat down when Gonzales left, and
my father spoke. "That man is charging an arm and a leg. I certainly hope that he's good." He spoke to me as if I were a business
deal that had turned bad, or a possession that needed to be fixed. All
of my life I had been treated like nothing but an extension of my
parents. I had their values shoved down my throat and had never
been given any chance for an independent thought or credit when I
had one. My own identity was so caught up in theirs that any indi-
viduality had been forgotten. If I did something wrong it was always, what will people think of us? not a thought for what really
happened to me, Susan, as a person, but what the meaning of my
act was as a member of the family. Now, even now, they thought of
their personal disgrace, of how sick I was, not what had led up to
this act, not how hurt I was. I wanted to scream, "It's me here in
jail, not you!" Then my father jerked me back with, "Well, Susan,
we came here to help you, but don't think that we have to do it.
We do it because we feel that you are meant for better things, and
that, with a little help, you too can become a productive and con-
tributing member of society. We do love you, dear. Mr. Cervantes
has been kind enough to arrange for an older man, a cousin of his,
an electrical engineer, named Mr. Castro, to look after you in jail
and make sure that you have everything you need. He lives in La

Paz. You look rather bad, dear, how do you feel?" I wanted to say that I felt like I always felt when I did something bad. I worried more about upsetting my parents than I did about myself. My family always had so much seeming emotion but all they really did was cover up on the outside, make sure that everyone thought that we had a perfect family, with no fights, that we lived in a veritable fairyland. Their reality had never made sense to me, so why should it now? I had rejected their life-style for twenty-five years, their reality; no one asked if you were happy or not, it was assumed that you were. No sadness was allowed in their house. So I looked and searched everywhere for anything just to get a reaction, just to get a little real hate or love, something real, for Christ's sake. I wanted to yell all of this, but instead I just said, "I feel very sick. I think that it's my ovary acting up again." And my father again, "Mr. Cervantes will arrange for you to see a doctor. Hopefully, they'll let you go with a guard."

It was so pathetic, my sentence, their stiffness, the smallness and ineffectiveness of my one-time giant of a father trying so hard, so that even he began to feel the pathos of the situation. He broke down slightly in his speech. "Honey, we know how long your sentence is for and we pray we can get you out. But we don't want, in any way, to be responsible for either Andrew or Ted, that means in getting them out. We don't even want you to see them, but what can we do about that? We are not going to stay here too long, only long enough to see that everyone knows here that you are not like Andrew and Ted, and that you have a good family. I brought you two books, *The Greening of America* and *The French Lieutenant's Woman.* We'll make sure that you see a doctor and that everything's all right."

Ernesto Duran came walking over and introduced himself to everyone. He talked to Manuel in Spanish and apparently explained the setup here, with the warden and the one judge. My father, aside to me: "Susan, as you know, I have never paid anyone off in my life and I don't intend to start now. I hope that I don't have to because of you." And finally my hysterical mother said, "Why, Susan, would you ever be attracted to someone like Andrew? He looks so weak. Oh, Susan, you are killing us, we came here because we love you, what can we get you, honey? We won't desert you." I thought, I chose Andrew because his looseness attracted me who was so structured, so rigid, but wanted to be free. Was pain something I chose to feel? I wondered if I had ever had an identity other than a negative one.

Since Laughlin had already bought me so much, and I needed so little, I didn't have much of a list to give my father. He questioned me intently about Laughlin. Who had sent him? Who was paying his bills? He made it very clear that he was angry that Laughlin had used my name in his efforts to pay off the judge's assistant. (I understood later, when I got my head together, that my father never paid anyone off and, furthermore, payoffs just wouldn't be of any use. One couldn't buy these officials.) Then, as Manuel Cervantes stepped aside for a minute to talk to the *comandante* about doctors for me and questions about my cell, my father and mother got to the nitty gritty of the visit. They wanted to know how I had gotten involved with such hoodlums. My father had had private investigators check out Andrew's and Ted's business and had found it to be phony. They could never understand, even after all my rebelliousness and my running, that I *always* chose men who were different from my father. They somehow tried to maintain the illusion that Andrew and Ted had seduced me away and convinced me to adopt their life-style.

"Mother and Dad," I wanted to yell, "I'm here because my life-style, Susan Beth Nadler's life-style, was not, shall we say, on the up and up. I was not influenced to join this merry band of smugglers, I wanted to be a merry smuggler myself." But their stiffness, their discomfort facing their daughter, the living proof of their failure to imbue her with their particular values, made me unable to be honest with them. Some vestige of their morality had been incorporated, unconsciously, into my values; I lied to them. My father asked me if I had invested any money in this deal. "Of course not, Daddy, that crazy I'm not." I told them that I had wanted to leave the day the package arrived, which was true, I had been sick, and they were desperate enough to believe anything. "Oh, honey, you mean that you knew somehow that you didn't want to get into this totally?" The question in my mother's voice pleaded with me to agree with her, so I did. I chose the easy way out, played innocent, let them keep their illusions—it would be easier on me. My mother thought, like Frank Zappa had said, it can't happen here, not to our daughter, but she knew in her guts. There I was in jail, for smuggling hash, lying to my parents who were trying to help me as long as I lied more and promised to go for their way of life. They wanted me to lie to convince them that I felt they were 100 percent right.

Andrew: I guess I deserted him that day; I knew that things would be easier on me if I didn't worry my parents with thoughts of him. I would be with him after they left La Paz, but the phony part of me, what belonged to them, would never let me see myself again as being a part of Andrew's world. After all, I had a B.A., knew a Monet from a Van Gogh, and wrote poetry. It is very hard to get to the core of your inner being and face yourself, just a little woman, with dirt in your nails and snarls in your hair and dreams. Mr. Cervantes had come back and talked to me for a few minutes. He seemed like a nice enough man, like the Mexican equivalent of my father, except that he was fair. He shook his head as he watched my father, and then he looked at me; I wanted to scream. I don't know why or how I went wrong, or what is wrong or right. Is smuggling hash wrong? Is deserting Andrew to save my ass right? I never really had my own answers to these questions. I was a reactor to rather than a maker of events. I knew only one thing: I was alone, my parents' values weren't mine.

I gave my father the list of things I needed in jail—razor blades, more Shalimar perfume, a hot plate, a coffee percolator, a new radio, books, pens, more paper and food, more deodorant. The list became more and more absurd as they wanted to get more and more things for me. We kissed good-by that late afternoon. My parents would go back to their hotel and plan things out for Manuel, they would send me dinner and come back the next day to bring my things and find out the exact charges against me. All would be well, and poof! like a dream they were gone and I was escorted back to my cell.

What was I doing here? I had grown up in a beautiful house with maids. I went to the ballet and ate Chinese food and my father never raised his voice; the only way I could ever tell if my father was mad at me was that he would make out my allowance checks to Susan *Beth* Nadler instead of just Susan Nadler. And I sat and sat on that filthy bed with Juanita screaming and wondered how one can ever hope to raise children if one has no idea or understanding of oneself.

The guards came and went, Ernesto Duran brought me dinner from my parents, steak, salad, vegetables, and ice cream. He also brought me a valium and a note from Andrew saying, "Tell them to go fuck themselves if they upset you, we don't need them." However, I did—I needed a small reality check to figure out who the dope-shooting, hard-talking, quick-witted, well-read woman in the mirror was. I was certainly no criminal. I found that after all the running and dope shooting and laughing and sunning and dismissing problems as bullshit vibes, that whether I was in jail or in Israel or in the movies or in L.A. health spas, *I* had no connection to whomever I appeared to be.

Oh look and see, all the fools who speak to me, and think I be. Oh look and see, the foolish me who things she's free. . . . See Susan run, through all the fun, Alone as she whispers.

*T*his chapter should rightfully be called "The Catharsis Caper," or "How I Learned to See, That Me, Was Not Where I Used to Be." I certainly can't call this a turning point, but I knew that I could no longer do whatever I wanted and count on the fact that it would be all right. Everything seemed to return tenfold to me. Right now, there is this pain in my stomach, and Tommy is at the door of my cell, "Susanita," with more mangos, and Jaime wants attention, and my parents are shattered because I broke the law, their law, their illusions and hearts, and how did I ever get this way?

Yeah, if you don't mind I just want to sit outside and talk to the bees, if you please. I'll call, I'm going to be late. God, yeah, His house is down the block, decorated by this fag, you see He had sort of lower-upper-class taste, too much French Provincial for Mom and Dad. No, they don't like His shoes, too pointy, occasionally one of the children asks God over for dinner, but mother needs at least a week to prepare for a dinner guest, even if He's blest. No God makes things too easy to understand, cuts out the need for the psychiatrist, I'd rather watch David Susskind. Please, Daddy, get me out of here. I'll do anything you want. I hate myself now, so vulnerable, at their mercy.

"Sure, Tommy, *muchas gracias,*" the mango was very good, you gotta eat. Mainly, I felt bad as Juanita clapped her hands, for a moment looked twenty years younger and kissed me good-by. The guard told her that I had paid for her release, she could not understand that I paid not because I cared for her so much, but just to have the cell to myself. She thought, nevertheless, that it had been a very charitable act. Thanks Andrew, thanks Ted, then thank Laughlin and the big boys in L.A. who gave him the money. Godspeed. Juanita, I felt bad, she would be back soon; she had learned nothing. It made me wonder if *I* would ever learn anything at all, or would someone always be there to bail me out. I obviously couldn't worry about the past now; if I had learned at all from my first bust, I wouldn't be in jail now. So what I have to concentrate on now is to be calm for my parents and to get dressed quickly. Ernesto Duran had stopped by to tell me that I was being taken to the doctor's, Manuel had worked wonders. I was being escorted by the *Federales* to the best gynecologist in La Paz, or as the police said, this side of the Rio Grande. I felt that my illness stemmed from my left ovary acting up, and I wondered if all of my life I was to be plagued with a cystic ovary, old karma, old wounds, mainly new-fashioned birth control pills that could guarantee that you wouldn't get pregnant, but couldn't guarantee that you wouldn't die of the side effects. The ends never justified the means, in modern medicine, machinery, or man. I went to the bathroom and washed, shivering from the chills of my own heat. I decided to wear my one and only dress, my Chino original. I pulled the dress on, slipped on my sandals and sat on the cot, to await the guards. However, instead of the guards, I saw the D.P. walking, with measured steps, toward my cell. He was carrying my notebook in his hand, my notebook of past days, hazy ways, and definitely negative evidence.

The guard stepped out from behind the building, opened my cell, and handed me breakfast, which I would have to eat standing up outside. The D.P. said good morning and all the social trivia, and that he wanted to meet my parents. I would tell them later that day, I said. Then he softly added, "Susan, this diary is impossible for me to read. There are many different persons' handwritings in it, not all yours?" "No, I did not write all of it." No sir, I should have added, that was Susan Z and Susan B; I had been so stoned, on so many days, that my writing had changed a million times. "Susan, you read it to me, I am interested." And I turned to the songs Andrew and I had written and read him the words, "In my life, I have prayed, to find one good man./Who could make, special magic, in his very hands./We could live upon a garden, in the stars, on the land./Moment to moment, kneeling together, a union in the plan." As I turned the pages and read more of the lyrics, I became sad for myself and especially for Andrew, who couldn't know that I now regarded my time in La Paz with him as so much self-delusion. I had reached a page entitled "Methedrine Madness," and as I spoke I very casually took the black felt-tipped pen attached to the notebook and blanked out "Methedrine," leaving only "Madness," which made more sense anyhow. Madness is madness is madness is madness. I proceeded through the book, crossing out all the incriminating words. And the D.P. was so into the words, and watching my mouth as I read to him, that he never noticed what I was doing. The heat was unbearable and sweat was dripping off my forehead, an hour passed and I kept reading, until the D.P. said, "Well, Susan, you are lucky. There is no evidence here. You may be a good girl." Thus I had another lie to live down. May they never know the real me. I finished and he told me that the *Federales* were waiting to drive me to the doctor's. I could keep my book, as far as he was concerned, and please ask my parents to call him. I took the notebook, put it in my purse, and followed him to the street. There were Adolfo and his brother Alphonso and two other armed *Federales;* they escorted me into their VW van that served to transport criminals. I sat down on one of the hot seats and tried to understand their laughter. The VW took us quickly through the town I was starting to forget. Soon we pulled up to a doctor's office and Adolfo escorted me into the reception room; there were no other patients, and the receptionist seemed prepared for me. Adolfo and I followed her back to the examining room. I left him at the door and walked into the room, feeling almost normal for the first time in ten days.

The doctor who received me was a short, stocky, older man who spoke flawless English. He treated me offhandedly, like the criminal I was in his eyes, and asked me some questions. I told him that I had had a D and C operation in Jerusalem, and an operation to remove a cyst from my left ovary in Pittsburgh in 1970, and subsequent chronic problems with the ovary. He weighed me in at 118 pounds, a little too thin for me he claimed, and I undressed for the examination that every woman dreads. After it was over, it was like every other appointment; he told me that I had a cyst on my left ovary about four inches in diameter, and gave me a prescription for an antibiotic. He called the jail, spoke quickly and brusquely in Spanish to Ernesto Duran, then told me that arrangements had been made for a Mr. Castro (Manuel's relative) to purchase my medicine for me and that I should, in the meantime, get Duran to get the prescription filled for me. He would see me in a week or so if I didn't feel better. In a moment of compassion he asked me if I could sleep, and I said no. He would order a prescription of sleeping pills for me if I wanted it. Not yet man, not yet. I don't really know why I rejected it, it was the first time I had rejected a possible high. I just felt so lousy anyway, I didn't want to be drugged out and groggy, especially now that I wanted to think. He said all right, good luck, and I found myself escorted by Adolfo back to the van.

There was much laughter as I entered the van and suddenly it dawned on me that the *Federales* all thought that I was pregnant. Very funny, Humor on that level, like slapstick, is the same all over. I sat quietly in the van, trying not to react or move too much. The heat was intense.

We arrived back at the jail, and the *Federales* escorted me to the room I always refer to as the waiting room. Ernesto was waiting for me. He told me that he would get my medicine for me, and that my lunch would be served in this room in fifteen minutes. He said that my parents would be here any minute with Mr. Cervantes to say good-by. Good-by? What the hell? They just got here. Then Ernesto told me that Andrew sent his love, I sent my love back, back to him who worried that I would be taken away from him, in thought only, by my parents. Not my parents honey, just myself.

My parents entered just then, stage right, my mother crying again, chic again, with Mr. Cervantes. My mother ran over and kissed me, I stood up and kissed my father, shook Mr. Cervantes's hand.

The first thing to be done was for my father to give me all my things
—my hot plate and radio and creams and foods and then $200 in
pesos, one half of which was to be kept by Mr. Castro until I needed
it. Then they told me that they were going to check out other lawyers, because Manuel felt that Gonzales was no good. I was offended, he was my and Andrew's lawyer. But I was not to say
anything: in a small town, like La Paz, you never knew if Gonzales
had connections with the judge. Then I told my father that the ol'
D.P. wanted to see him and he told me that he had no time, this
trip, to see either the *comandante* or the D.P. My mother said,
"Susan, you see the main thing is to get a retrial for you, alone, separate from Ted and Andrew. We want you apart from them, they're
bad news, and in Mexico, if you keep seeing them, the judge will
think that you're guilty. So stay away from Andrew, stay by yourself." It was as if a blow had hit me; Mother, some part of me loves
him. I knew I would see Andrew all the time until we were forbidden to by the law, but I sure wouldn't tell *them*. My father said,
"Susan, you have to build up a good image of yourself." (Isn't it a
little late for that, Daddy?) "We are going home to regroup, as it
were, get some money, and find out if the Senator from Pennsyl-
vania can help us and also clear up this Innerclean mess. Do you realize that you are being held on charges, not only of smuggling
hash, but possessing hash capsules? A real mess."

Then the real feelings started coming out. My father's eyes looked
misty as he held my hand, my original old man, and told me not to
worry, they were doing all they could for me. They knew how tough
it would be, but I should call if I could, call Mr. Castro if I needed
money, and write. I can't remember much of what was said, only
that for the first time since I had been busted, my parents looked
and acted as if they worried about me stuck in that jail, not about
themselves trying to save face in their community. I knew that in
their heart of hearts, they really loved me; they were just unable to
act other than their way. The time flew, they had a plane to catch,
they loved me, be strong, you too. And I kissed everyone good-by.
Then, a rather heavy mistake was made. Manuel got permission for
my father to carry my things back to my cell. I told him it wasn't

necessary, but he insisted. He carried everything in his arms, the way he carried me when I was a baby, and we, accompanied by a guard, headed back. My father saw my little tree, sign of life, in front of my cell, it was in bloom, and then the guard opened the door. I thought that he would faint from the smell, he acted nonchalantly, he put all my things down on that lousy bed, and then Jaime screamed for me and I tried to explain how sorry I was and for one minute he held me and then the guard told him he'd have to leave, and he took a chocolate bar out of his pocket like I was a little girl and gave it to me, saying, "Keep your chin up, honey," and then the guard locked me up. I watched my father disappear, and his walk was slow, and broken, like he was crying. I sat on the floor and ate the chocolate and cried for everyone, I cried until my eyes were slitted and swollen and I couldn't see the image of my father. Then the guards changed and brought me dinner from Andrew.

My dinner was long over, I had rinsed out my clothes, hung them up to dry, and taken my "buckets" early. I felt like all the crying had cleansed me, somehow. Duran brought me my medicine, which I was to take twice a day for ten days. Andrew sent me a note telling me that in two days, on Sunday, I would be able to visit him and that Laughlin had written Ted that all was going well, whatever that meant. Jaime had cried and I had played the recorder for him, and now, at nine o'clock, all was quiet except for the noise from Tony's TV. Thanks to the dictionary, I had picked up a few words and was now able to communicate with Tony. He had told me that he would be in jail for two years; then he was going to San Diego. He'd never really explained why he was in jail. I had candles lit and was under the sleeping bag reading *The Greening of America,* feeling cozy and secure. Suddenly I heard Tony call through the hole in the bathroom wall. "Susana, Susana, come, important." I put my book down and walked into the bathroom. Tony and I had worked out sort of an agreement—he would let me stop up the hole when I was in the bathroom and then, when he was very lonely, we would take out the gum and toilet paper and talk. It seemed very urgent. "Susana, the vigilante come here, rape you." What the hell was he talking about? "Susana, rape you, one hour, the vigilante." What the hell, did they have a fuckin' KKK here to get foreigners? "Me Tony, I here a long time, I know truth. Trust me." For one minute reality passed me by, and I thought vigilante, what, is he crazy? Which I knew he was. However, he was my friend, I mean I gave him cigarettes and candy and we laughed together. Then he started again, "One hour, rape, poor Susana parents gone today." How the hell did he know unless he had inside information? "Susana, no one else help just Tony. Listen." I started to hear voices outside, a lot of them, and I became absolutely frantic. I lay down on the floor, and started to shake. Why not raped? Perfect timing, my parents leave, who would care if I were raped, no one, and the voices grew louder, "Susana, good-by, rape." And Tony was gone from the hole. I was lying on the bathroom floor, helpless, in pitch-black darkness, and trembling. Oh my God, raped, and for what? I whimpered that way for at least half an hour, then Tony again, "Susana, fifteen minutes." I absolutely froze. I heard lots of men's voices outside the cell, and I felt hot urine, my own, running down my leg. I had heard of people losing control of their bladders in fear, but I never knew it could happen to me. I started to rock. Tony made sounds like he was crying. Ten minutes passed and the cell door opened. I tried to hide on the floor. My life started to pass in front of me. I started to scream, Tony started to laugh. The light went on in the bathroom, and I screamed as loudly as I could. It was the *comandante*. Jesus God, was he the head of the vigilantes? He looked at me and I looked at him and from the other cells we heard laughter, and I incoherently tried to explain to the *comandante* what had happened. "Susan, tonight holiday. Party. We bring you one piece of cake. Tony is crazy Susan, don't listen to him. Cake on the bed, you crazy too," and he left me there. Tony was laughing hysterically, I was still shaking. I wanted to yell at him, what good would it do now? Then Jaime woke up and started to scream, "My darling, my darling, I will help you!" Tony had known that the police would be here tonight and he also sensed my fear, and so had decided to play a "joke" on me. I hated him; I also hated myself for believing him. It took me two hours to get up, undress, and get into bed. I ate the cake, it was good, and I started to think. I felt drained, tired, and nervous. I wished again and again that someone would hold me and reassure me, but wasn't it time that I reassured myself? I should be strong now and on my own. My hands hurt from lack of using them. My heart hurt from being pulled apart so many times. My head hurt from all the worry. My mind had probed, or at least begun to probe, what it's like to be insane.

*F*riday isn't pay day and Thursday night doesn't begin the week end when your life-style is free and unstructured. Everything is a week end. Those are the days when you throw away your watch and lose track of time. You may still have a doctor's appointment on Tuesday to remember, and unemployment-office day on Wednesday, but you are not rushed, nor does your life center around vacation. Why should it? I had never worked regularly. A great day of accomplishment sometimes was to wash my hair, pick up the all-important mail, and go to the cleaners. I noticed that in foreign countries, where values and schedules are different, I always lost track of what day it was. The only thing I knew for sure was the weather. So the days in jail began to be confused with each other; I knew that on Friday my parents had left, and that Sunday I would see Andrew, but I began to think in terms of the day after tomorrow instead of the date.

It was Saturday when I woke up, I knew this because everyone else, the guards and visitors, such as Tommy, did not appear on schedule. Tommy didn't work on Saturdays and the week end police force was composed of different men. As I groggily opened my eyes, I realized it was early, 5:45, and that the sun would soon be coming up in all its glory. I looked at my tree and realized her blossoms had fallen off and her summer garb of green leaves had replaced them. I looked past the tree and saw the fifty soldiers leaving the jail in two trucks. What a waste of men! Ever since Laughlin had left, the army had guarded the jail like a revolution was to take place. They must have been very bored. The four morning guards approached my cell, opened the door, and walked to the heavy metal door; they opened it and entered like real heroes to let Jaime, Tony, and Felix free to play in the courtyard until six o'clock in the evening. I knew that, simultaneously, Andrew's and Ted's cells were being opened. The guards smiled at me as they eased out and locked me in again. I got up, shook out my sleeping bag, and turned on a James Taylor tape—a little throwback to the old realities; then I walked into the bathroom and was jolted back to the night before and Tony's scare. It became like a thousand other incidents that had happened since my being busted and incarcerated—stored up and useless in my present situation. I couldn't really blame Tony, only myself for having fallen for it. The first person at my cell was Ernesto, bringing me breakfast and new containers of distilled water. I could never drink, brush my teeth or even wash my dishes with the water from the pipe.

They had installed a new sink the day before but I wouldn't use that water either. I assumed the *comandante* had it put in to impress my parents, but unfortunately, despite its immaculate white bowl and brand-new pipes, it didn't work.

Ernesto gave me a long note from Andrew. It started out by telling me how much he loved me and how he understood what I had gone through with my parents. I was skeptical, but realized that Andrew deserved credit for understanding universal emotions, such as guilt. Then he told me that Gonzales had been to see him and Ted and had told them about my parents and how much he was going to charge them. He had put in a petition with the judge to get a retrial and it had been denied; the judge felt that we were guilty and if we wanted a retrial we would have to go to the appeals court in Hermosillo. The whole procedure, due to the usual Mexican slowness and legal technicalities, would take at least six months, or so he suggested. Six months to put in an appeal that might be denied! I felt absolutely beaten before I had even started to fight. However, Andrew assured me that Gonzales had a lot of connections and would do everything possible to speed up the process. Andrew obviously had a lot of confidence in Gonzales, as did Ted, and I more or less trusted their judgment. At that time I thought, unfairly, that the reason my parents didn't like him was because he wasn't sophisticated, and I had to trust someone in this situation. I knew that I loved Andrew, but trusting him and his big men in L.A. in this deal had landed me in jail, so I would have to think this through slowly. Andrew went on to add how ridiculous the Innerclean affair was. My life rested in the hands of an incompetent chemist. He said that maybe Gonzales could have the tabs taken to Mexico city to be analyzed. Then he went on to tell me how Ted was falling apart and crying all the time. I could definitely dig it, Ted really had the most to lose, he was playing the part of innocent victim, and one word from either Andrew or me and he would be in big trouble. However, for Andrew or me to cop to this truth would implicate us, since we were both working on the premise that we knew nothing about anything. Oh Andrew, poor baby, comforting Ted and worrying about me. My thoughts were interrupted by a guard who motioned that I was to come with him to the *comandante*'s office, *muy pronto*.

I wondered what the problem could be; maybe he wanted to discuss last night's scene with me, but I doubted that. I put on a pair of cut-offs and a little halter top. I knew it was an outrageous outfit for jail, but it was so hot that I was more worried about comfort than about the way people looked at me. Six months in this hole to await the decision of the judge for a retrial in Hermosillo would kill me. I walked out of the cell, following the guard, and was amazed at the beauty of the earth and sky; Baja has virtually no pollution. The guards all whistled and made me feel uncomfortable, but I think if I had been worried about what they thought I would have worn a raincoat. As I walked into the *comandante*'s office I saw Andrew and Ted also waiting to go in. I ran up to Andrew and hugged him tightly. "Hi, honey, and hi Ted." I really started to feel sorry for Ted now, he was very pale, had lost more weight, and his coloring was atrocious, especially under his eyes, where it was greenish black. "What's going on Andrew, what's the story here baby? Why are we being taken to see the *comandante?*" Ted spoke first, "Maybe we got a pardon, maybe we're free." "Jesus, Ted, the *comandante* can't pardon us. Andrew, do you think he wants us to give a concert?" But even as I spoke I knew that the *comandante* would never call us in especially for concert preparations. Andrew spoke quietly: "Honey, why are you so distant? Detached? I know this ordeal is tough, but we better keep it together. I promise you that when we get out I'll take you to Northern California and we'll settle down on a few acres of land. This whole ordeal is a big test for us, to see if we really are strong, can't you dig it?" "Andrew I don't think this is a test at all, it's more of a lesson to make us stop and think where we are really at. All this talk about karma and good vibes and us full on in the divine, and here we are, caught trying to smuggle dope, to buy land to go to be spiritual in another place because we obviously couldn't do it here, and all we ever did was get high. Where are we going, do you really think anything could change us?"

Then Adolfo stuck his head out of the *comandante*'s office to motion us in. Our conversation had been cut short, but two expressly different points of view had been offered. I looked at Andrew and he at me and he knew that not only was I starting to question the integrity of our love, but also the integrity of our so-called life-style. Adolfo escorted us into the inner sanctum. The *comandante* was dressed in slate gray again, his face disgruntled and red. I remembered not to be afraid. We three lined up in front of his desk and he addressed his first comments to me. "Susana, you know the *Playboy* magazine?" (No time for me to answer.) "Well, in Mexico, it is called *Ella*. Their reporter is here to see you, interview you." (What is this, me alone? A pin-up stint, Susan the convict.) Andrew said quietly, "Oh yeah, I saw this dude pull up in a white Jaguar, very duded-up looking." "Andrew, you quiet, I talk to Susan alone." Poor Andrew, the *comandante* had such animosity toward him, he thought he was the original brains of the deal. "He come now Susan."

A man, or should I say dude, walked into the office. He looked like a short, stocky Mexican, which he was, who had poured himself into a pair of pants, which he had done, made for a thin, lanky

American, which he wasn't. He looked decidedly uncomfortable. He had on a thin, flowered shirt, carried a leather bag, and wore his hair long. He introduced himself as Jerry, and spoke hardly any English. The *comandante* was watching everything very carefully. Jerry spoke first to me, after scrutinizing me from head to foot, "Susan, lots of money, pose for pictures. We pay." I interrupted him, "Listen, Jerry, I am not interested. Andrew, please tell him in Spanish for me that I am not interested in posing and if he wanted me to pose alone, why did he ask that you and Ted be here for the meeting?" Andrew translated, Jerry answered and told him, "She is very, very pretty, the Mexicans are interested in women. We wanted you two men along to help her make the decision." Andrew then informed him that he, as my fiancé, was not particularly interested in having any more publicity for me. Ted had been very quiet, intensely so, then he leaned over and whispered to me, "This stunt stinks, I wonder what he really wants?" I was about to tell Ted that he was too suspicious and paranoid when Jerry, under his breath, murmured, "You speak Yiddish?" I was so taken aback by this that I almost fainted. Yiddish! I looked at Andrew, he looked at me very quickly, Ted's hair stood up, Jerry continued, "I am from the Jewish underground, we come to help you escape." Suddenly, to me, he no longer sounded like a Mexican, but a full-on Israeli. Were these our people coming to take us out? It was too bizarre. How did he even know that we were Jewish? Andrew looked like Richard Chamberlain, tall, thin, blond, green-eyed; I could have passed for an Arab, Italian, Spaniard, Greek, Mexican, *or* Jewess, you know, man, ethnic, very ethnic, and Ted looked like a chicken. This whole situation was just a little too much, especially since Andrew answered him in Yiddish. "O.K., so how are you going to help us?" he said. Jerry started to answer so quickly in Yiddish that I cracked up, I mean, this was definitely off the wall. The *comandante* got suspicious and yelled, "Susan, what speaks Andrew?" I said to him, "This is not bullshit, man, he speaks Yiddish." The *comandante*, began to get angry, and said, "Pish, smish, go back to the cells at once!" Jerry made a beeline for his white car, with the *comandante* yelling at him. I was laughing hysterically, the guards grabbed me and took me away, Andrew said he'd see me tomorrow, and Ted gave me the peace sign, baffled.

Back at my cell, I tried to piece together what had happened and eventually gave up trying; we never did find out if the dude was from the Jewish underground in Mexico. Lunch came with a guard, it was beans and vegetables and rice and cake, it smelled delicious. I felt very strange, extremely nauseous, and couldn't eat at all. I knew that I was getting sick, but with what? The whole situation was just outrageous. I took my medication and started to write Andrew a long letter, but I never had time to finish it; it was like I was the most popular girl in school, guards never stopped coming to see me. Another guard walked up to my cell and opened the door, motioned that I was to follow him. I grabbed my purse and found myself escorted by four armed *federales* to the VW van again. This time I asked no questions. Adolfo, in his inimitable way, kept saying, "Smile, baby." O.K. man, I know that things could get worse, although how much more so I shuddered to imagine. We drove much longer this time, and I recognized many streets. One we were on was the romantic ocean-view street that housed our favorite restaurant. There was a man selling ice cream, I knew that word in Spanish; funny, you always learn words for the things you like the best. Adolfo stopped the van, got out, and bought me some. I tried to pay him, but he wouldn't let me. The van soon pulled over to the side of the road and we all got out. It was about three o'clock in the afternoon and everyone had left the streets to sit on their porches for siesta. They stared at me like I was a side show. We walked into a photographer's shop and I panicked. Were they going to force me, at gunpoint, to do a naked layout for that magazine? But a little old man walked up to me and shook my hand. His studio was filled with portrait shots of families and weddings and children and dogs. His little dark eyes were intelligent and comforting. In perfect English he said, "Come with me, Miss Susan, I have to take a picture of you for jail, what they call a mug shot." I felt really sick to the stomach, a mug shot. I had thought that somehow I was going to avoid all this TV reality of bookings and records. Me, Susan Beth Nadler, being booked; it hurt me almost as much as seeing my father walk away from the cell. The man was trying to be kind. I felt very low. "You like my work?" he asked me gently. "I love people. You have very sympathetic eyes, it will be a pleasure to photograph you." Adolfo looked out from behind the black curtain that served as a backdrop, I sat on a little stool, and the old man pinned my number, my booking number, onto my little shirt. I was humiliated: numbered, tagged, snapped, posed, snapped, reposed, and humiliated. I never looked that dear little man in the eyes. When it was over, he said to me, "You like the beach, I saw you there many times swimming. I will tell the police to take you there on the way back to the jail. Good-by and God bless you." He unpinned my booking number from my T shirt, and I walked, with lowered eyes, back to the van.

The old man spoke to Adolfo and his brother, they seemed to agree with him. The van headed down toward the beach road. The sea was out there, beckoning. Once she had spoken to me and called me in, now she seemed so out of my reach. When we reached my old haunt, Coromel Beach, the van turned down the road that led to the sand. When we arrived there, the door opened, and I bounded out. Quietly, Susan, don't go too quickly, you'll scare them. I walked with four *Federales* and their machine guns, past the concession restaurant and the fish soup and raw fish cocktail. Everyone there knew me and nodded hello. I walked past the very few brave enough to sit in the sun, kicked off my sandals, and ran into the water up to my thighs. I felt so good, the *Federales* were all drinking beer, which was not allowed—I guess everyone needed a break. I played in the water and felt chilled, but wouldn't get out. I danced and sang hello to the waves and felt foolish, it was another crash with the real world. I thought of the night before as I lolled in the water. Night fright, another night of tears and fears. I hadn't been able to sleep or eat, too nauseous. I know that life can be beautiful, but I also know that all the world suffers. The Mexicans say that hope is the last thing to die in man. It is true. We cling tenaciously to life, despite the problems, we want just one last chance to dance the joyful steps, spread our arms, and embrace the day as I embraced the water. It was thick here, all thick, tropic vibes, many new facets of life revealed. I liked the people in the tropical countries: I liked life, I missed it. I walked dejectedly out of the water, picked up my sandals, and the *Federales* accompanied me back to the van. Adolfo, when we got in, said, "No one, no one." I knew that he meant tell no one or we would all get in trouble. I said, *"Sí, sí,"* several times, loudly.

Later: I was marched back to my cell. It was nearly six o'clock, and the town was preparing for Saturday night. Cafés cleaned up, restaurants prepared lots of tortillas, bars cooled many beers, young girls washed their thick hair and put on white blouses for their boy friends, musicians warmed up their instruments. I ate dinner alone, shivering. The music outside haunted me.

12

Sunday morning I slept late, like I did in my high school days, when, after a hectic week end, Sunday was the morning of rest. It was about eight o'clock when I got up, and realized that I had slept through the six o'clock visits and Jaime's good-morning-darling yells. Lately I had been sleeping very fitfully, sweating profusely, and not dreaming. All the days had begun to blend into one nightmare. I hurt to the core, I ached, I ached, I was self-centered.

Then I remembered. Today was the day I got to go over to the men's side and be with Andrew all day. I jumped out of the sleeping bag and turned on the radio. The Beatles were singing "Let It Be," which was applicable to me and all of you, wherever you are, who try to change or control situations that are not in your hands. "Let It Be" was followed by a commercial for tanning lotion—Oh, I remembered the day before on the beach. My tan was fading, slowly, but I was not so much concerned with the absence of the tan as I was with my yellowish cast. I had washed my hair the night before, and it was still damp. It pulled it back in a rubber band, determined to look my best today. I washed and put my mirror on a bar in the cell door. With sunlight streaming in, I carefully put on some eye make-up for the first time in two weeks. I felt much better, more feminine, and better equipped to face all the men when I was finished. Then I went into the bathroom and practically tripped over the breakfast the guard had left for me; I got dressed, all the time wondering what the men's side would be like.

The family-visitation plan of the Mexican penal system is much healthier than our less liberal system in the United States. Women and children get to visit twice a week, couples can make love, although no one really talks about that aspect, the single men can buy a prostitute for a day. Homosexuality is very scarce. I walked over to the bed to make a list of the things I wanted to take with me to the men's side. The recorder topped the list, then the tape deck, songs, colored pens, a radio for Andrew, shampoo, and some books. I looked out the door and saw about fifty women approaching the cell, headed by Juanita. For a minute I thought they were all being put in with me, and then I remember that today was Sunday. Never on Sunday. Today was the day the prostitutes got checked. Juanita skipped up to my cell, and presented me with a single rose, a bottle of cold beer, which I quickly hid, and a box of candy which I later gave away to Tony, Felix, and Jaime. She had tears in her eyes, and kept thanking me, again and again. Then she introduced me to all of her sister coworkers, Gina, tall and blonde, Carmen, dark and fat, Rosa, Tamara, Margarita, the list went on and on. Each one smiled and said in Spanish, "With much pleasure," or "Pleased to meet you." It was very touching. Juanita had one of the prostitutes who spoke English well ask me how much longer I would be in jail, how I felt, and if I was going to see Andrew today. When I said yes, they all giggled and made the universal sign for sex. The doctor approached the examination room, which was next door, all the girls became serious, and lined up. No more smiles, just intense facial expressions, and when one of the girls came out a cheer if she was clean (free from VD) and a boo if she wasn't. They seemed to have a real camaraderie and sympathy for each other. When a guard approached, they all turned their backs on him and swore. The checkup was quick; all the ladies were examined and given either a clean bill of health or determined contagious within an hour, and then laughingly, with arms around each other's waists, they disappeared into the streets.

It was about 9:15 by now and I was impatiently awaiting the

guards. All the time I kept thinking of something I learned in a comparative literature course. In *Crime and Punishment,* Dostoevsky speaks of the few criminals, prostitutes, and insane folk who leave the normal boundaries of behavior and jump over the wall that surrounds society and accepted behavior. My parents' arrival and their impact on me had started to change my ideas. I felt safe inside this wall and in my cell; I had only my thoughts and actions to justify. I could somehow pretend that everything would be all right because I was changing. But once I stepped into the men's side where there were real criminals, I would be faced with the fact that my changes and subsequent honesty, at least at this time my partial honesty, didn't make me any better than the others, nor did it mean that I would be saved. I would have "stepped over the wall" and out of normality. It was all mixed up in my head and very complicated. What it meant, aside from my nervousness about going over to the men's side, was that I was nervous about the self I'd meet over there. It would be very easy to talk to Andrew and slip into the old routine of, "Well, we're covered, we're divine Brother and Sisters of the Light, smuggling dope isn't bad, God will get us out." But I knew this wasn't true. I also knew that it would be difficult to explain this to Andrew. He would think that it was because my parents had influenced me, and that I was rejecting our shared, very funny, values. He would not be able to understand that I was questioning *all* values; my parents' influence on me only made me question *their* values.

Then I saw the guards approaching the cell and my heart started to race; they opened the door and I picked up all the things I was taking over with me. They looked me over, noticed the eye makeup, and indicated, by their laughter and gestures, that I was getting pretty for my man. Before I could be taken over, however, I had to go to the little examining room and be examined by the woman who occasionally acted as a matron for female prisoners. She checked all my possessions, my wallet and purse, and frisked me quickly. I imagined that she was checking me for dope. She examined all the women who came to visit their husbands or sons or brothers or fathers that way, in case drugs or tools for escape were being smuggled in. Then, with two guards flanking me, I was escorted into the reception room. There, the warden was checking out all of the visitors. There were at least fifty people waiting to go in. There were wives, girl friends, daughters, sons, friends, uncles, aunts, mothers, fathers, sisters, brothers, a few animals, and a lot of food. The people were all poor, and dressed in the clothes and colors of the earth. The colors were very pure, hot colors of jasmine, oranges, bananas, mangos, pineapples, grass, and trees. These people could not seem to contain their feelings of jealousy or hate or disappointment, emotions we are taught to control at a very early age. Greed was also an emotion of theirs, on a rather small level, but nevertheless there: therefore they did not judge me. They felt that somehow we were all part of the same trip.

I got in line with the rest of the visitors and waited as smothered conversations took place and I felt heat and warmth with these people. Most of them knew who I was, for my picture had been smeared on the cover of every sensationalist magazine in Mexico. Most of their men had commited crimes far more heinous than mine were thought to be. Walking in beside me was the man who had, so many warm afternoons, sold me *orchata,* or rice water, a Mexican drink. Andrew and I usually made a stop there on our way back from the beach. He was a tall, hawklike man who always looked me in the eyes. In his manner he had always understood that Andrew and I were slightly smashed. Now when he saw me he was trying to feign ignorance of who I was, although I had probably conversed with him thirty-five times. He could not look in my eyes. I watched him carefully, probably he was visiting his son or nephew, avoiding my eyes, with his hands in his pockets. I stood next to him in line for at least twenty minutes, silently. Just as I was supposed to go into the prison, he stopped, looked me directly in the eye, and handed me a glass of rice water from his plastic thermos. No talk, no recognition, just a glass of rice water. I respected his respect for me. These men were definitely not used to seeing a woman in jail. I saw him again many times after that in line to enter the men's side, and in the prison itself. He often spoke to Andrew, but never spoke to me. I never tried to break down his double standard. He never gave Andrew a glass of rice water. He never spoke to me.

The line slowly moved up to the door that led to the courtyard that was surrounded by the cells of the men. When it was my turn, I walked in slowly and stopped to look around. Andrew was not there to greet me, so I thought I should just keep walking. Under their gaze I felt myself moving rather sensuously. They had read about me, heard about me, and seen me on TV. I was the first American girl to ever enter the men's side of the prison. The values here were not like the old get-the-criminal values of the *comandante* and the *Federales,* nor like the values of the people who slowly make it through. These men knew that they had lost to the law their freedom, families, and fun, yet also all their responsibility. They all wanted out, but were not in any hurry. The courtyard had benches and a basketball net. Andrew had told me that he exercised here. I looked into the cells—they were small, having once been hospital rooms, but furnished with collages, pin-up pictures of Jane Fonda and Brigitte Bardot, a few beds, radios, TVs, hot plates, wall hangings, murals, and other unexpected things. The men apparently lived a lot more comfortably than the women; of course the men were expected to stay in much longer because of their crimes, which were always punished more severely than women's in this macho society. I passed by Chino's cell, which was private, and saw him merrily sewing away on his machine, which they permitted him to keep. I passed by the kitchen. Louis was there cooking for his family, who had come to visit. There were long tables where some men worked with abalone or conch shells; they designed jewelry, trays, and other oddities that were sold outside the jail and the profits split with the warden. The men were apparently not robbed of their dignity or virility. Most of them were poor, odd-job men but their prison work seemed to have some meaning to it—they were not forced to do work that was demeaning or exhausting as far as I could see. Suddenly, Andrew stepped out from one of the cells and surprised me. Another crash with reality. "Hi, honey, glad you could make it, come on in and see my apartment." I kissed him hello and walked into his cell. It was largish and slept four men. They had rigged up a curtain to separate themselves from the other four-man cell directly across from them. Andrew opened the curtain and I walked in and there was Ted, lying on one of the beds. I walked over and kissed him hello. He looked worse than ever. "Hi, Susan, how are you doing?" And then he started to cry. Respect or no respect, I felt very sorry for him. I understood exactly how desolate he felt; he couldn't sit there and pretend his big-time friends would get him out, nor could he play the big man. Andrew looked at me and knew that I fully understood the condition that Ted was in and also that I would be very kind. Ted was crying very hard by now and chokingly said, "Susan, do you think we'll ever get out of here? I can't understand why they're holding us." I said to him, "Ted, we'll get out. There really is no evidence to prove that we're guilty. However, don't forget that we're in for a reason, because we *are* guilty. In Mexico the law even defines us as guilty until proven innocent." Ted immediately hushed me, "Susan you never know who's listening. Be quiet. For all intents and purposes, we're innocent. Oh Christ, I promise if I ever get out of here, I'm goin' to live so clean, so clean . . ." And so it goes, I thought. We all want to atone for our sins and maybe we'll all have a chance. What I was starting to realize about my life was that I did not want to be like Ted. I was so bored with myself and my inadequacies.

I turned on a tape for Ted, and Andrew and I walked out of the cell, to leave him alone with his misery. Andrew spoke first. "Honey, thanks for being so good with Ted. He's really been down and out. He's so guilty, he's so afraid of being caught. He's afraid he's going to lose Loretta. I try to help him. Listen, let's you and I walk around the place, pretend we're visiting friends, and forget what we're doing here." (Andrew, how can we ever do that?) "Anyhow, honey, I got some food together, some bread and milk and butter and maple syrup, I kind of promised everyone that you would cook some of your great French toast. Then later, we can go to Obidon's room, he has a single, and we can be alone for a while. Honey, you look awfully yellow. What's the matter?" I felt rather lousy just then, and aside from that, I wasn't exactly into cooking for the whole prison. Oh well, what the hell, I might as well enjoy myself. To Andrew I said, "Nothing wrong Andrew, I just haven't been feeling well lately. Probably nerves." I had given in, decided against the talk I had thought to have. It's hard to change so quickly. Amen.

So Andrew and I, arm in arm, we tried so hard to act as if we were just taking a constitutional around a friendly village. Andrew started to explain about the jail. "You see Susan, as I'm sure you observed, this jail is very lax. At six in the morning when we're let out of our cells, we can do pretty much as we please. We all get to talk to each other, play basketball, and work at what we want to. The whole system, much as I suspected, is oriented around money. You pay the warden for what you want, the *comandante* supposedly doesn't know about this payoff system, but who can tell? He may take all the money from the warden. It's so crazy here, I can't ever tell what's going on. Anyhow, Ted and I weren't supposed to be together in one cell, they're afraid of escape. But a few dollars to the warden, and it's taken care of. If we want special food, we pay for it, we pay the warden off, give Ernesto a little money, and he gets it for us. A few pesos to the warden and we'll each have single cells, very cool, huh baby?" "Andrew, I know this might sound strange, but it's so corrupt, haven't you had enough corruption?" Then I thought that all corruption had become the same to me. My parents' lies to their friends, my father's lies to the lawyer, telling him I had never been busted before, my lies to my parents about never having invested money in the deal. How could I live in this world and maintain myself? And then Andrew, "Listen Susan, don't suddenly get so high and mighty, a few pesos is what's keeping us happy, would you deny that?" I couldn't answer, I didn't know, what the hell can you say when you're in jail for corruption? We continued on and I was introduced to the abalone workers; Andrew was having them make a barrette for my hair. I met the goldsmiths and the silversmiths, stopped to thank Chino again, and ordered a macramé poncho from the worker who made them. Then Andrew introduced me to the cell-block heavy, Obidon, a huge man, about twenty-five, very muscular, dark, and wearing an earring. He was one of the only people in for murder. However, since it had been in self defense, and only over a woman, it was excusable. He had a single cell, got whatever he wanted, and lorded over the other prisoners. He and Andrew had become friends. I never trusted Obidon, he had violence in his eyes. He spoke with us in street English for a while. I asked Andrew if he could hear me when I yelled to him during the day. Obidon told me that my bathroom wall was on the other side of the courtyard. Why didn't I drill a hole in the wall so that I could talk to Andrew every day? It was such a great idea, so much better than notes. (We still didn't know that the *comandante* had every one of our notes read to him before we received them.) It was risky, yet it seemed like such a great idea compared with paying off the guards. We would have the freedom to talk to each other every day, whenever we wanted to. I decided to do it, the adventuresome spirit in me identified digging a hole in the wall with a "great escape." Obidon, who knew all the tricks concerning the prison, told me that the walls were very soft; he gave me a long nail to push through with. We three decided that the best time to dig was late in the day, around six, when the guards were drilling. It would muffle the sound.

I had come over to talk to Andrew about my changed feelings, how I felt about jail, and why we had been busted, to tell him that I really wasn't like him or Ted or the Susan he knew, or like my parents, that I was afraid and tired of hiding in dope, music, and paranoia. I had come to say all of this; I ended up digging holes in walls. Somehow all my good intentions had flown away. I had no excuses. We left Obidon's cell with an extremely long nail stashed in my sandal. I would start work tomorrow at six. Andrew was hungry and I decided that I would cook French toast for everyone. We went back to the cell and found Ted much better. The other two cellmates came in and I met them; they were both young boys, cousins, in for smoking pot. Ernesto came in bringing all the food; it was like a party. I beat the eggs, added the milk, and started soaking the bread and frying it. I cooked French toast for what must have been an hour and a half. I cooked up three loaves of bread, which is a lot to make in one pan on a single-burner hot plate. Ernesto took some out to the warden, who asked for seconds. Andrew made coffee, and when all the hullabaloo was over, we finally ate our food with Ted. It was now two o'clock, siesta time, all the children were sleeping on the floors, the husbands and wives were resting in the sun. Obidon came over and told us we could use his cell and that he had a surprise for us. Andrew and Ted and I walked over to his cell and sat down. He closed his curtain and locked his door, smiled a big smile, and produced two very small joints for us to smoke. I became absolutely panicky. I had smoked alone, in my cell, when we had first been busted, but I was not prepared to smoke a joint now, on visitors' day, with a stranger who might be an informer. I tried to indicate this to Andrew, but he either didn't notice or didn't want to notice. Obidon lit up the joint, they passed it around, I took one hit and said I didn't want any more. I was waiting for the police to bust in and bust us again. Everyone got ripped, not having smoked for a while, then Obidon and Ted left Andrew and me alone.

There was so much I wanted to say. I needed to tell Andrew how I felt about everything, especially us. Andrew didn't want to talk, he wanted to make love; I wanted to scream into the hard stone walls and dank odors; I wanted to run into the ocean and feel it kissing my thighs; I wanted to open up and show Andrew my inside parts that were confused. Obidon's cot was hard and lumpy, outside, children cried in their sleep, flies buzzed, the air was hot with passivity. The prisoners had all they could ask for, who needed more? I looked over Andrew's shoulder and saw a picture of Ché Guevara, Obidon's hero, a revolutionary who had been cruel and brutish, shot down in his early years. We made love with our shells. I was distant and could not experience the golden glow of other beds. It was more like an effort to reassure ourselves that we still were alive, not totally chained. But my heart belonged to the Andrew of weeks ago, confident, carefree, and laconic, the Andrew who lived with the Susan who never knew that to talk is easy, to do and really believe in it, is extraordinary. Then, I had loved him because I had loved myself, now I was suspicious of my dreams and could not respect someone who loved me, or that particular me. When it was over, and Obidon's alarm clock went off indicating that he would be back in the room soon, I pretended that Andrew and I were on a raft floating down a river, that we couldn't get off the raft or we would be consumed by alligators or drown. Yet we couldn't stay on because we would starve and be beaten by the elements. So we clung to each other and waited for a miracle to rescue us. I knew then that if I told Andrew that I no longer believed that our love was capable of existing without drugs and pipe dreams, he would be deeply hurt, and that when I got out of jail, which would probably be before him, his life would be absolutely hollow.

We walked back into the courtyard and the sun hit us hard, draining what remaining strength I had left. All the eyes were upon us, the Chinese, somehow sardonic eyes of Chino, the eyes of Louis, the cook, the proud, defiant eyes of Obidon, the gentle, timid, brown small eyes of Andrew's cellmates, all the passive, resigned eyes of the men who knew that jail gave them security of sorts and the excuse not to work for their families; and the tired, tired eyes of the women, their thick eyelids, so weary of their lives. Then I looked for Andrew's eyes, but the sun was too bright and I could only see where his eyes should have been. Ted's eyes were frightened, like a rat's. My own eyes I couldn't see; I didn't want to, I knew I had a long way to go before I could look into my own eyes and not be disappointed. The air was stale until the late afternoon breezes cleaned and refreshed it. Andrew and Ted and I sat on the ground in the courtyard, singing, and trying to be friends. I would see them for sure on Thursday, maybe they could pay the warden off and we could be together before that. Yes, my food was fine, the doctor had given me pills, we would be free. Six o'clock came and despair led me out of the men's side and back to my cell. My gray stone chamber was cold. Where was the golden sun of the other side? I was here, alone, with my own eyes, the smell was terrible. My dinner was brought to me, a special dinner from Louis, with ice cream for Susanita. No TV tonight in the jail, Sunday, the holy day of the Father, the Son, the Holy Ghost, the Virgin Mother, and all those who suffered for a cause they believed in. That was the terrible part, I was suffering for something I didn't even believe in, couldn't even define.

Jaime cried out for me, he was angry that I deserted him all day for "that *bandito* Andrew. What does he give you that I can't, the wind? The sun? The stars or the moon? Your freedom?" And he laughed so evilly at me that I picked up the recorder and played a new song I had learned from the Mexicans, "La Paloma." Jaime was quiet, Tony cried so slightly. I played "La Paloma" again and again. All the notes began to sound the same. Music was always in my soul, music was in my heart and on my lips when I arose and went to sleep. It made things so much lighter. Mexican music however, was so passionate, thick, and sensual. I played a few verses of "Old MacDonald," purely for native reasons, and cried myself to sleep. I felt lost, suspended in time, like I was part of an animated cartoon. I couldn't remember what I had done three days ago. I was totally lost, on another planet. My only reality was jail, all else was gone.

13

*T*he following morning was the hottest day I'd experienced in jail so far. Not only was it hot, it was overcast and exceptionally humid. I woke up with a terrible fever, very depressed. To spend twenty-seven years in jail, with nothing to look forward to but Thursday and Sunday visits with Andrew! I wanted to be able to walk outside and smell the heavy air, I wanted to be able to get up in the morning, make my own breakfast, and go for a walk. Mexico is so overpoweringly passionate, the colors are rich browns and greens and blues and reds. The flowers don't give out a calm odor, like tulips; the jasmine and gardenias are intoxicating. The eyes of the people are so honest, they are not condescending, like the eyes of the Israelis, or hard, like those of the Americans, they are more like the eyes of the Arabs, slow, hot as the sun, evasive as the sand, and solid, very solid. These eyes look at you directly, past your class, or your clothes, or your jewelry, they penetrate into your heart of darkness. Simple transactions, like buying fruit in the market and rice water at the corner, become an intimate eye-contact communication between yourself and the vendor. I remembered all this.

This early Monday morning, beginning my third week in jail, Tommy came to the cell door, accompanied by an old couple that looked like matched raisins, the man shriveled and brown and toothless and barefoot, the woman shriveled and brown and clean and barefoot. Tommy kept repeating that they were his parents and their little heads bobbed up and down in the heat rising from the ground. The old woman put her hands into the huge folds of her brown dress, and slowly, with a widening grin, pulled out fresh dates and peaches swollen with ripeness. Her husband kept bobbing up and down, and from underneath his spotless white shirt he pulled out a prayer, forever bound in plastic, in Spanish, with love from Jesus. They pointed to the sky and tears fell down the woman's face and she grabbed my hands through the bars and loved me with her fingers. Tommy stood back a few paces and smiled benevolently, as if he was the parent and they his children. He was as proud of them as they were of him, and I was to be a part of the scene. They crossed themselves many times, kissed my hands, and the three of them then held hands and walked away into the heat, their mission accomplished. Bring a little religion to the heathen *americana* who looks so innocent. My breakfast arrived but I couldn't eat it; I felt hot and then cold. I took the medicine the doctor had prescribed, hoping that it would work. After I drank my coffee, I sat in the cell and realized that I had nothing to do that day, nothing to look forward to. My parents were gone, I wouldn't see Andrew for three more days, I was alone.

I would have to start to find ways to amuse myself. The cleaning man came to the cell and I stepped out to enjoy the air with my guard. I sat down underneath the tree and looked out into the street. The Mexican people walked so slowly, no one hurried. Maybe it was the heat that slowed them down, or maybe their acceptance that everything will get done that should get done. The old man was done in my cell, and I thanked him for his help. Lately I had need to communicate with all the people who were so kind to me. I had fumbled around in half-Spanish, half-English too long. The time had come to try to learn Spanish. I had only a dictionary, but the real way to learn a language is to talk to the people, which I would, and necessity is the mother of invention, as they say. The guard locked me up, but I had a purpose, something to interest me. I took my diary and made a schedule for myself of how my days would go. Get up, eat breakfast, write a note to Andrew, clean the cell, study Spanish for two hours, listen to tapes or radio, eat lunch, siesta, wake up, play the recorder, talk to Tony and Jaime, read, watch the guards drill, watch the sunset, eat dinner, read some more, write letters, take a shower, rinse clothes, and sleep. Sometimes, when life seems very aimless and meaningless, the only saving grace is rigidity. I not only was in jail for twenty-seven years, in a foreign country, I really had no idea of who I was or what I wanted, except some peace of mind, some feeling that I was not just an aimless particle, but part of some order. Therefore I tried to impose order on myself. I also wrote in that I would play solitaire. I had no idea on how to go about learning a new language. I had studied French for six years, and Italian for one semester, but paper and practice are very different. I decided to start out mainly with nouns and not worry about the conjugations of the verbs. I wanted to learn practical words like food, distilled water, cell, judge, lawyer, guard, music, fear, day, night, sun, moon, clean, dirty, parents, guilty, innocent, basic simple words. I felt so relieved when I was done; I was able to organize something. I loved to organize, it made me feel that everything was in its right place, and secure.

The other task I had in front of me was to drill the hole in the wall of my bathroom. Obidon had been insistent that I dig at night, when the guards were practicing drill, but I wanted to check things out. I walked into the bathroom, crouched on my heels Arab style, and picked at the wall. It was thick, but not that thick. I could hear muffled cries from the men's side. The composition of the wall was very loose, and pieces flaked off when I scraped it with my nail. It wouldn't take too long; I would start that evening. Tony and the gang had the radio on very loud, and they were screaming "Susie! Susie!" as usual, and I answered, this time in Spanish, *"Sí?"* Tony hurried to turn down the radio and started to tease me about the vigilante. "Susie you cry, vigilante." I wished that I knew the word for asshole in Spanish. He asked me for a cigarette. I sat on the floor, my dictionary in my hands, and quickly thumbed through until I found the word for how many, *"Cuántos?"* Tony replied, *"Cinco."* I knew that this was "five." Somehow, as insignificant as this conversation had been, it pleased me. I slid ten cigarettes under the door and Tony started to laugh hysterically. Jaime had been quiet for several days; I thought that maybe he was in a coma. I'll tell you, I felt more like *I* was in a coma. It was getting hotter, and I picked up *The French Lieutenant's Woman* that my parents had brought me and started to read. I read for two hours, the sweat falling down between my breasts and forming a pool of liquid there. The story was time-consuming as opposed to interesting, but it kept my mind off my own personal tragedy. Reading became the opiate of my days, filling me up and lulling me into a reality where I had no need to cry or shake, my senses were not my own. I was thankful for this break in intensity. The guards yelled back and forth to each other, the cars passed outside the front of the jail in the street, perhaps seventy-five yards away, yet there was no real noise, all was blanketed in the heat and lethargy of Mexico. The heavy air absorbed the noise and put it away inside the vapors that rose from the trees and sand, the streets, the animals, and the dark people.

And so my life passed for a few days, absorbed in the heat and passion of the air; rise, eat, study, read, music, cry, sleep, eat, read, shower, and at six each evening sit in the bathroom on the floor and pound the nail into the wall with my wooden shoe. Progress was slow but steady; when done for the evening I would stop up the hole with toilet paper; it blended in with the gray of the walls. Andrew would write to me of love in the afternoon, freedom in the evening, and land and trees in the morning. I would write of ideas that were colored orange and deep green, of values long forgotten and of guilt, red as the sunset. My Spanish was progressing, I was delirious with organization, three thick days passed with little interruption, and suddenly it was Thursday and I was to visit Andrew. I was almost afraid to leave the noiseless shelter of my world and go to his, but I was saved from making the decision.

Thursday morning the *Federales* came to get me and took me into the jail. I was dressed and ready to see Andrew. Adolf smelled of Old Spice, his mustache precise, his gun polished. He took my arm and showed me my mug shot on the wall. It was up alongside Andrew's and Ted's. Who was that dark-eyed girl, so indolent? I denied any knowledge of her; I didn't recognize her. Her arrest number looked slightly, only slightly, familiar, the two men whose pictures were with hers were perfect strangers. I was insulted to think that the *Federales* thought that I knew them. I felt feverish, flushed, and out of this world. Instead of joining the line of visitors, I was led outside and next door into an old building where an old man in an old sombrero sighed, a sigh older than he looked. He had a block of ink before him and about fifty forms, each one with my mug shot on it. Adolfo was left to guard me, and the others went to drink beer. The fan on the ceiling spun around and around, the room was red, old red. I held out my fingers and watched as he pressed them into the ink and pushed them down five times on each sheet; ten prints per page, fifty pages, five hundred fingerprints. I couldn't believe they would take so many. I would be late for Andrew. My Thursday had been raped, the old man was gentle, he had no teeth, just some stumps, and was chewing tobacco.

We established a rhythm, dip, center, put down, push, push, push, push, push, now the index finger, and so I was fingerprinted. By the time I was done it was one o'clock and Adolfo's clean linen shirt was drenched with sweat. He marched me outside to rinse my hand in turpentine. Then we slowly walked back to the jail. The warden opened the gate to the men's side and I was allowed to enter. I felt like I was walking down a street of small houses, in each yard children played or slept, families sat together and drank and ate. Short, dark men and fat women with long greasy hair and pink bows in it, sat eating tortillas and shooing flies off their thighs. I walked by quickly, they all watched me, I came to Señor Andrew's house, knocked at the curtain, he opened his heart, we talked of many things that day. We talked of how Gonzales was an excellent lawyer and would get us out soon, we talked of what our lives would be like on our land, we talked of how we each felt. No, I certainly didn't hate him for anything, no, I knew that he didn't do anything on purpose to hurt me. I never really told him, though, *exactly* how I felt, I now think because in some way, aside from not wanting to hurt him, I was weak, and clung to him; I was afraid to be totally alone. So I only intimated the changes I was going through and opted for the superficial, keep it together on the outside. He wanted to make love, I was too hot. Ted came in, green, and we formed the gleesome threesome. They were telling me not to be afraid, better days would come soon, we were protected. Andrew told me to go back to the doctor's, the pills weren't working. I fell asleep and dreamed that I was walking down the beach, alone and naked. Suddenly I saw a huge tidal wave coming, it was coming slowly, I had time to escape. It was a huge wave of blue and green. I started to run, I ran down the beach, my feet never moved. I started to cry, the wave was coming, I woke up. Andrew was telling Duran to make sure that I got to the doctor's. My time was up, I left the cells and all their visitors, very dizzy. I was escorted to my cell, the guards were getting ready to drill. I pounded the nail in the wall in time with the sergeant's yelling. The hole was getting deeper and deeper. Andrew had been excited, I had shown him where it would come out. Two more days and it would be done. I was exhausted and had the chills. Ernesto brought my dinner with a guard and told me I was being taken to a laboratory for blood tests the next morning, he had received orders from the *comandante;* he also told me that both Andrew and Ted were worried about me. I was distant, he gave me a valium. Didn't he know that I could hardly hear him? The heat was absorbing all the noise, there was only silence. I slept.

The next few days were distant, noiseless, and feverish. They were without name. I would mostly sleep, and wake periodically to eat or dig at the bathroom wall. The day I went to the doctor's was indeed surrealistic. I woke late, around 9:30, and it took me some time to establish where I was. I had missed the early morning guards, Tommy's visit, and my breakfast, which sat in the corner of the cell. Several tendrils of long hair were plastered to my neck with sweat. Ernesto bopped up to the door with a newspaper article featuring the gleesome threesome and orders to get dressed immediately. Somehow I couldn't move. I felt sticky and drifting, and where was Andrew? I glanced at the article, so many magazines in Mexico are sensationalist, the media know the educational level of most of the people so they write exaggerated and almost porno articles about deaths and rapes and police victories. The poor people, with hardly any diversions from the heat and hard work, read the oversimplified stories that give them the thrills of experiences that they will never have. There was a picture of me with my hair pulled back taken the night I had been busted and questioned. I was smiling sardonically, and looked like a spy. The caption stated that I was twenty-nine, from India, head of a Mafia ring, and lived in Chicago. Again, they capitalized on sex and drugs. Susana Nadler, who likes only sex and drugs. Poor girl, I thought, I wonder who she is? Andrew's picture made him look sleazy and insipid, Ted looked, unsurprisingly, like a chicken.

I got dressed in my Chino original, minus the Band-Aided nipples, and waited for the *Federales.* Adolfo appeared at the cell, looking dapper, and was followed by the guard, who let me out. The heat was blinding, my Spanish faded, and I was escorted into the VW and driven to town, to a spot across the street from the post office. Everything, places and faces looked so familiar, yet so changed. I felt, for the first time, that I was in the presence of a foreign culture. I didn't belong here in this languid, passionate, yet resigned world of slowness, siesta, and squalor. The laboratory was in an old house, overgrown with ivy and jasmine. Two old raisin people sat on the front porch, the man held his beaten-up hat in his hand, looking at his toes, which protruded from his sandals. The woman's thick black hair was held high on her small head, her dress was reddish brown, like sandy soil. She made clicking noises with her tongue when she saw me being escorted in by two armed *Federales.* I could hardly hear anything; I existed in my own feverish bubble world.

It was very clean in the office. Two nurses in white lab coats, clean shoes, and clean fingernails greeted me, they touched my arms, their eyes were brown. One told me in broken English to wait for one minute, my guards sat on either side of me. Adolfo came in with an ice cream cone for me. My friend. I thanked him in Hebrew, confused. The nurses came to take me into a back room just as I picked up an old *Time* magazine. They sat me on a table, moistened my arm with alcohol, and took several tubes of blood. The procedure was easy, I knew it well. Then they smiled at me and said good-by. The guards stood up as I re-entered the room, and we walked out. I looked across the street to the telephone booth I had stood in so often, and was amazed. An old acquaintance from Pittsburgh was there, so it seemed, making a call. I started to yell hello, but the guards hustled me into the van. This touch with my old world was gone.

When I came back to the cell my lunch was waiting, along with a long note from Andrew. I couldn't eat a thing. The note told me how Gonzales was making good contact in Hermosillo for an appeal trial, and it went on and on about legal procedure. I fell asleep reading it. When I awoke it was late and the guards were drilling. I rushed into the bathroom and began banging the nail, until it came through on the other side; I was filled with fear, but I hit it again and again until I could see through the hole. There was the men's side, roll call was going on before the men were locked up for the night. I could barely make out Andrew and Ted. Suddenly the drillers stopped and so I went back into my cell and heard Jaime scream for "Angelitos Negros." I put the tape on but felt so hot that I lay down for a minute. The next thing I knew it was six o'clock in the morning. I couldn't remember what day it was. The guards said hello, I saw them as very small, in a fog almost, walking quickly and jerkily. Tommy appeared at the cell door with candy and bread, but I couldn't get off the bed to greet him. He smiled, as if to tell me he understood. He didn't, he yelled, *"Amiga, amiga,"* several times. The next thing I knew I heard Andrew's voice coming from the bathroom wall. He was standing directly in front of the hole, with Ted. I felt so close to him, lying there on the floor in that goddam bathroom that I started to cry. He told me to get it together, that Ernesto had heard from the warden that the results of my blood tests were back and that I was very sick. He told me to pack up all my things. Mr. Castro, Manuel's friend, would store them. I was to be taken to the hospital. I didn't believe him, but he insisted. Simultaneously, Ernesto appeared at the cell and called me. He told me to hurry, but refused to tell me what was wrong with me. I began to pack everything into my sleeping bag and suitcase, including the clothesline and the cleanser. The cell door opened then, and the police threw in about eight women, headed by Juanita. She was drunk and didn't recognize me. I recognized all of the women as prostitutes from Sunday, they screamed like birds, no one seemed to notice me. I put all my things together on the floor and sat on them. I was glad that I was leaving. I couldn't have made it with these wild women. The small cell could never have contained all these souls. They were screaming and ripping each other's clothes off. A fat one stood at the cell door naked, her huge breasts and black nipples hanging through the bars. She kept hitting her breasts on the sides so that they swung back and forth. A guard, an older man, appeared; he was bringing my breakfast and when he saw her breasts, he turned red. All the prostitutes clamored around her and exposed various parts of their bodies. The guard would not open the cell for fear they would run over him. Still, none of the women seemed to notice me. After the guard disappeared the women quieted down a bit and some squatted on the floor and urinated. I was starting to feel sick. Juanita walked over and defiantly grabbed my breast, but what she really wanted was my shirt. She said, "Me. Me." I hit her hand away and she looked angry. I wondered how long it would be until the guards came to get me, and prayed that Andrew wouldn't call me through the hole. The prostitutes were of many colors, and of all shapes and sizes; I felt very small and helpless. However, no one had bothered me but Juanita, who finally left me alone. Andrew called me through the hole and I tried to tell him not to talk because of the women, but he couldn't hear me and kept yelling. I was afraid to leave my things in the room, so I lugged them all to the bathroom and told Andrew what was happening. The women saw me and started twittering; they pushed me away from the hole. I was saddened, dizzy, feverish, and soon very distant in my soundproof bubble. They pushed me farther away, and tried to force their asses or breasts in the hole. I walked into the other room, heard only silence and the faint, faint pulsing, pulsing of my blood. Soon, the guards came for me, and carried my possessions out of the cell. I looked in as they pushed the prostitutes back and saw I had forgotten a tie-dyed mandala on the wall. There it would have to stay in the dank smell of urine and feces.

The warden had me sign my weekly paper that said that I was an inmate and entitled to receive three pesos a day from the government. Andrew and Ted appeared from the men's side, because of special permission and a few pesos to the warden. Mr. Castro, an older man, took my things while Andrew held me. I was being taken away from a jail, but also from all that had become familiar to me. I asked what was wrong, but no one would talk. Finally Andrew told me that I had typhoid fever. I think that I started to cry. I asked Ernesto to please contact my parents, I asked Mr. Castro to contact my parents. Ted kissed me and gave me the peace sign, it was so funny and pathetic that I started to cry and laugh. Andrew was talking, but I couldn't hear a thing. Everyone had started to look like characters from *Gulliver's Travels*. An ambulance with two *Federales* was waiting for me. Was I going to die? I saw the jail, Andrew, and my beautiful tree for the last time, then fell asleep in the ambulance. I have been so many places, alone.

14

*T*he ambulance came to a jerky stop. The *Federales* got out, machine guns poised for action, and I stepped into the sweltering heat. The Hospital Salvitorre was a modern, multiwindowed structure that looked very familiar to me. Lounging everywhere on the grounds, seated on cement benches, underneath green-goddess trees, were the *gente,* or the people of La Paz. Apparently, this hospital served as a sort of park or resting place for the poor of the city. They were really there because things move so slowly in Mexico that the people sleep and eat outside the hospital while waiting to be examined at the clinic, or while visiting relatives. It was so relaxed on the grounds, little children slept or played in the grass, old men talked quietly to each other or slept under newspapers, wives brought cold tortillas and refried beans, husbands joked with each other and watched pretty student nurses walk in and out of the hospital. It reminded me of the jail on visitors' day. As I walked by with my two guards, the people all stared. Some smiled or waved. Everyone had sympathy for the underdog, and no one could believe a girl as lovely as I was a criminal. These poor, gentle people became my friends and my support during the three months I spent in the hospital.

The corridors were very clean, so different from the jail where all was dirty. Young interns dressed in white passed me in the halls and smiled. Some said hello. I could not hear a word, I could barely see, I felt as if my feverish bubble was floating by them all slowly, oh so slowly. We stopped in front of a door marked *Señor Dr. Cardoza: Hospital Chief.* One of the *Federales* knocked at the door, removed his sombrero, and entered; Adolfo stayed with me. In a moment the door opened and I was motioned into the inner sanctum of the head doctor. I was expecting to see an old, frazzled, white-haired man, bent over his work. Instead, a young man of perhaps thirty-seven or thirty-eight, with a round, clear face, dark hair and eyes, and glasses, greeted me. He spoke perfect English. "Susan, I am Dr. Cardoza, head of this hospital. Dr. Van Borstel, your doctor, has ordered you here for treatment of typhoid fever and a possible ovarian cyst. You are under his care, but the legal officials, and the *comandante,* are in control of your confinement. You will be put in the detention cell, which is designed to accommodate sick prisoners. I think that you will find it considerably more comfortable than your jail cell. Meals will be brought to you three times a day, the room will be cleaned. However, the *comandante* has ordered that you are to remain in solitary confinement. You look terrible. Yellow, jaundiced, much too thin. This is the result of the typhoid fever. We are not pleased to have you here. We do not like criminals, especially drug smugglers. We understand you are guilty, we understand you and your boy friend lived very well, had a maid, and lots of money, and you had no visible source of income." I felt my bubble forming again. Things were growing distant, but I realized that to get along in the hospital I would have to be on good terms with the Chief. I would have to lie to him, play on his pity, to be considered innocent. I hated the position I was in, I would have to live two lives.

Yet I liked this man, these people. I would fight for my false innocence. "Dr. Cardoza, don't you think it a little presumptuous to judge me guilty before you know my side of the story, or before you know any of the facts other than the slanted ones presented by the newspaper? For a man who seems educated, your sense of law is slightly provincial. I am not guilty and I consider it an insult that you never even bothered to find out my side of the story. Now, if I could trouble you, I would like to place a long-distance call to my parents to inform them of my condition." "Susan, the lines are out again. They have been so for one week. When conditions improve I will notify you. And please, excuse my quick judgment. It is just that I am so anti-drug. I saw how much damage they can do when I worked in the Mayo Clinic for seven years. Now, I will be back to talk to you later." So that's where he learned his English.

Float, float, I started to float again. I won with him, my sins will surely be revisited upon me. But what could I do, admit my guilt and be treated like what I really am, or perhaps am not? Things got more confusing as I tried to rationalize my lie. We left his office and continued walking down the corridor. The slatted windows let in delicious breezes, trees were everywhere outside. We reached the kitchen and made a left down the corridor. Suddenly I stopped. Across the street was the apartment I had lived in with Andrew. I felt for a moment as if I had lost my grip completely, as if this building were a mental institution. And so it was to be for me.

My detention cell was at the end of the hall. It wasn't too large, but it had two beds, a bathroom with a shower (My God!); and a porch, more like a wooden box, with wooden bars on the top through which the sky could be seen. My section was far removed from the rest of the hospital, and next to it was an old T.B. ward that had been abandoned. Superstition usually is high among uneducated people, so I suspected that the guards would be afraid of ghosts. (This suspicion proved to be true.) I was very tired and feverish at this point, and put all my things on one bed, then sat on my lumpy mattress. There was broken glass all over the floor, and the windows were knocked out. Adolfo stepped in and pointed at the mess. He indicated by gesture that Jaime had been in this cell and destroyed everything. Poor Jaime, when would they take him to Guadalajara clinic? The door to the room was a regular cell door, and it was now being closed by Adolfo. He then locked it. I soon passed out, oblivious to my surroundings.

When I awoke it was after six and I was sweating profusely, Dr. Cardoza was entering the room with two student nurses and an old man with a broom, mop, and cleansers. Another old cleaner. Dr. Cardoza had me step out into the hall with him. "Susan, the *co-mandante* called me. There are going to be two guards always here with you. Not *Federales*. I will have your room cleaned now, the student nurses will make up your bed and give you a hospital gown. Dr. Van Borstel will be here soon with medication. The long-distance lines are still down. If you need anything have one of the guards contact me. Good night and good luck." I looked at my two guards and became furious: one's name plate read Loretto, a fat, quiet man of thirty years. But the other was Alberto, the guard who had tried to get me into the bizarre sex trip with Juanita. He smiled at me vaguely, made a gesturing sign with his hands, but I didn't return the smile. The old man had swept up the larger pieces of glass and haphazardly cleaned the bathroom and floors. I put all my creams and shampoos in the bathtub, turned on my radio, and waited until the student nurses made my bed. They gave me a hospital dress and I went into the bathroom and put it on. I looked like a snowflake with slight overtones of yellow. I got into the bed and the girls took my temperature. (Most of the nurses in the hospital were students who could not afford to go to school to become regular nurses.) One of the girls was very fat, with dark hair—short and curly with a bright yellow peroxide streak down the front. Her eyes were sky blue and her mouth never stopped. "Susanita, I am your friend Connie. You are sick, I help." And she giggled. I liked her. The two guards walked away from the cell to the hall, where they sat down. The thermometer was in centigrade, I took it out and quickly realized that 39.8 degrees was about 104 fahrenheit. I was drifting off again. The girls fluffed my pillows and tried to get me to eat some rice and potatoes, but I couldn't eat a thing.

My doctor appeared. I hadn't seen him in two weeks. "Susan, you are very sick. We are going to take blood now, and you're going to take these antibiotics three times a day. It is better here, no?" I couldn't answer, just dozed off as he took more blood from my arm and gave me a shot. I fell asleep and dreamed of blue eyes that turned to green and were Andrew's eyes that had dollar signs on them. I dreamed that peasants led me out of my cell to a church formed in the shape of a cross, clean and white. And my dress was red and flowers were in my hair and we all knelt together in prayer and I flew away into the sky, which was the ocean, writing Spanish with my hair in the waves. The Spanish turned to Hebrew and stones rolled on me, and my father appeared, my gentle father with his high forehead, and I dreamed he was on top of a hill crying softly, the world lay at his feet, he was filled with sorrow for a world that had failed him, and his tears were ivory and I fell slowly to his feet, where I crawled. I woke up suddenly, nauseous, and found that I had urinated in the bed. There were two nurses with me. I had somehow set my alarm clock before I had faded away. It was 4:30 in the morning. Connie was there; she told me not to worry and took my temperature, which was now about 105. I felt like I was swimming in sweat and urine. She changed my sheets and dabbed water on my lips and I thanked her.

Different guards were in the hallway in front of my cell. They had come on at six o'clock, when I fell asleep. The shifts were from 6:00 A.M. to 6:00 P.M. There was a small, fat, little guard with a mustache and wondrous eyes, he had a little red-and-white bandanna around his neck. He was wiping his forehead nervously. At his side hung the smallest pistol I had ever seen; he was very proud of it. He saw me look at him and he winked. We were friends forever more. I dozed off again to nightmares of Death, who wore red, white, and blue and looked like Uncle Sam, but he had horns and danced above me with a pitchfork that turned into a hash pipe. I woke again. It was ten o'clock in the morning. A cold breakfast sat beside me, and the guards had changed again. I got up and went to the bathroom, washed with cold water that wouldn't get really cold. Then I sat in bed and wrote a note to Andrew, telling him what was going on. I gave it to one of the guards and tried to tell him to give it to the warden to give to Andrew. I never knew if the guards understood me or not.

All day I drifted around my room. Sometimes I found myself on the ceiling, other times looking up at myself from the floor. No one came, the door was locked, the floor was still covered with glass, dirty sheets lay in a heap. A new nurse came to take my temperature and give me medicine. She was afraid of me and wouldn't talk. I slept again, it was terribly hot. Six o'clock. I wanted to turn on the TV for the news, then remembered where I was. The guards changed. Alberto was back. He looked in and pointed to the trays of uneaten food and dirty sheets. He held his nose. I slept again, in misty vapors I walked with my mother. She had on a long white dress, her hair was all white, her eyes the color of Connie's. I begged her for forgiveness. She spoke to me in Yiddish, and I drifted. I woke, took medicine from Connie's hand. She fed me ice cream from Adolfo who stood outside my cell and smiled. She was gentle. The next day, the room was filthy. Trays lay everywhere. The little guard was outside my cell sitting at a table. His feet didn't touch the floor. He was unwrapping an old cloth that held aromatic tortillas. He rubbed his little hands together with glee, with the joy of life and food. I got my dictionary out and looked up the word for clean. It is *limpia*. I said to him, *"No limpia aquí, no limpia."* I startled him; he jumped up and smiled at me. I begged, "Doctor Cardoza, Doctor Cardoza." He looked at me with compassion and left his food. He returned fifteen minutes later with Dr. Cardoza. I said, "Doctor, aren't there sanitary conditions here? No one cleans my room or takes away my dirty trays. I am so afraid. Am I dying?" He was stern, but said little. "I will get a boy who will clean your cell every day. I will tell the women in the kitchen to remove the trays. They are afraid of you. A criminal. No, you will not die. Typhoid fever is serious, however. It will take you a while to recover." He left and told the guard that someone would come to clean the room. The little guard smiled, and said, *"Sí, sí,"* very respectfully. The doctor left and in ten minutes returned with an awkward youth. He had thin, yellowish skin, slicked-back hair, buck teeth, a wispy mustache, and a smile as gentle as rain; his name was Salvatore. He would be responsible for dusting, sweeping, and washing my floors and bathroom every day. He looked at me and I knew he was a friend and that he believed in me. When language barriers come up it is easy to learn how to read eyes and hands.

He began to sweep the glass out of my room very carefully, he gently lifted up the bed to get under it, and got under all the chairs and suitcases. He smiled the sleepy, resigned smile of the Mexican poor and I wondered how old he was and if he liked to drink or dance. Then Dr. Cardoza brought back a very thin, dark, wispy leaf, named Juanita; I think I had an affinity for women of that name. She wore the yellow uniform of the nurses' aides, Salvatore wore the sky blue jacket of the maintenance men. They smiled at each other, but she was afraid of me and quickly picked up the trays and left. Dr. Cardoza remained to ask me how I felt. The little guard stood at attention at the doorway, longingly looking at his food, yet interested in anything that happened. Dr. Cardoza told me that the orders were that I was to be locked in every day. There was no way the door could be opened. I was a prisoner, that I knew well. I wanted to change the subject, so I asked, "Doctor, why is an intelligent man like Jaime locked up in the jail? Why can't you keep him here?" The doctor answered, "We kept him here. That is why all the glass is broken, Susan. He is a catatonic schizophrenic. He is a very intelligent man, but he must take medicine every day. When one of his fits comes on he starts to drink and neglects his medication; then he is uncontrollable. He was a student with me in the university so we made appointments for him at the Guadalajara clinic and they give him shock therapy. This seems to help." I was opposed to shock therapy as I had read so many negative things about it, how it alters states of consciousness and humiliates the patient. To Dr. Cardoza I said, "But isn't there something else they can give him or use? What about chemotherapy?" Dr. Cardoza looked at me and asked, "Where did you go to college?" "I went for three years to the University of Wisconsin and took my degree in Jerusalem." "And you read a lot, Susan, I can see from the books here." "Yes, I like to write too and if you ever have a chance could you please bring me old *Time*s or *Newsweek*s?" "Yes, I will." He started to exit but just as he was leaving asked, "How did a nice girl like you ever get involved in this?" And I thought, Oh, it's worked. He was impressed by my intelligence and concern for humanity and I realized that though all this was true, I would still have to lie my ass off and pretend great innocence to get sympathy. The situation forced me into a position so that I would have to feign innocence; like I had been duped. And although I knew I would never betray Andrew, I wondered how much I would have to betray myself. I was so tired of lying, and I knew that part of my karma, part of all this, was payment for thinking I could make money on something I had never worked for. Part of this lying and cheating karma was that I would have to cheat and lie to make my story convincing. I would climb on lies like on a stairway to the stars, however intricate and illusory, till I wouldn't be able to tell to whom I lied about what. My stairway was shaky, I felt humiliated. Fear of myself had always been my mind-killer; I had never been able to love myself because I was always so dependent on my situation, not my real being. Now it was time for me to try to learn to love myself, because I realized that I was just another human being, with faults. But the general idea was to be constantly aware and attentive toward myself so that I could change myself with love, because the only way to do something is to realize what's happening and treat it peacefully and with a gentle hand. Fear is a little death that finally brings about total obliteration. I now had to face my fear, see it for what it was, let it pass in and out of me. When it was gone, I could trace its course, see where it went, there will be nothing in its place except a stronger me. I had to try to have discipline, and not be concerned with "winning." I had to be a woman. I had here a perfect opportunity to change and find myself, if I could make it through the lies and the switch of values, seeing as that is what ultimately would get me out. The lies that would get me out would be far worse than the lies that got me in.

The little guard locked me in and sat down to eat. When I awoke little Juanita was bringing in my tray and my medicine, apparently given to her by the nurse. The air was very still. I smiled a still smile at her, she scurried out. The guards changed, the room was white, I was all alone in this clean cell, in my white dress, in white sheets with my pale white skin. I truly felt as if I were in a mental institution; solitary confinement can make you feel that way. I wrote another note to Andrew, but I was much more careful in what I said. I had a feeling that before it reached him, it might be read by the doctors. I wondered what the date was and suddenly knew that in two days it would be June 18, Andrew's birthday. I had given Ernesto 100 pesos before I left to get Andrew a sterling silver chain for his neck, and I had also arranged with one of the male prisoners, whose father was a baker, to get him a cake. I would miss the celebration. I knew the bust was not his fault. I thought how difficult it must be to be a man. Andrew really didn't have enough faith in himself to try to work. He had no sense of himself, no idea of the feeling of achievement, how it makes you feel. So smuggling seemed like a good idea to him. I wrote him that I understood; I thought in my head that I could never live that way again. I wished him a happy birthday, rather ironic. Happy twenty-nine years of unproductivity and dope, baby. I finished the note and called Alberto over to the cell. He wouldn't come at first. Finally, he made it. I gave him the note and one for Ernesto asking if everything was O.K. Alberto was very nervous around me.

I sat on the bed and held my head, tired from all the mental exhaustion of trying to think clearly. I felt hot and cold at once: the typhoid fever blues. I dozed off again. At ten o'clock I woke up again. There was a lot of commotion outside my cell. The lights were on in the hall, apparently Alberto's sergeant had come in to check to see if everything was all right. Connie came in to take my temperature; it sounded like everything was echoing through a loudspeaker. "Susan, open wide, wide, O.K., O.K., O.K., O.K., O.K., O.K." The next thing I knew it was morning and the third set of guards was there. These men, who were to become such an integral part of my life, were dressed in khaki uniforms and hats. Then the routine started. Juanita brought in my breakfast of mush around eight, and Salvatore was let in around ten, with his sleepy smile and his brooms. I walked out to the porch, but the heat was too intense for me. The nurse came in to change my bed and give me a clean gown. Finally everyone left, and I lay down on the bed, exhausted. Suddenly the guard appeared with a strange little man. He had blond, crew-cut hair, beady gray eyes, was dressed in a black suit with baggy pants, and a starched white shirt, his tie looked like a shoe lace. He was American. I was transported by a single man back to the phony super-sophisticated atmosphere of New York, Pittsburgh, Brooks Brothers, Bergdorf's, the lovely life of mouth sprays and deodorant, onion smell forbidden, pale faces with expressive eyes straight out of Revlon. As he spoke, the guard opened the door and I sat, "Susan, I am the American Consul from Tijuana." I sat up more quickly and got off the bed to shake his hand. "No, no, don't touch me." He raised his hands high above his head and repeated, "Don't touch me. You might have anything." The guard was very alert, brought the man a chair, locked him in, and stood guard at the door. "Now I don't have much time, Susan. It's probable that you'll be here in jail for at least fifteen years. Now, now, it's not so bad here. I just left your buddies, Andrew and Ted. They send their love. Andrew gave me these magazines for you. Now, don't even breathe on me, dear." He adjusted the string on his neck. I couldn't believe this. "Apparently you have a good attorney. The hospital isn't so bad here, I've seen a lot worse. Now fifteen years isn't so bad, is it dear?" and he smiled that insidious little smile. "We Americans can't worry about you in jail. Your own problem. However," he got up to leave, "if there's anything you need, why, you just let me know." He called for the guard in Spanish and before I knew it, he was gone. Like the Lone Ranger, only how could I contact him if I never knew his name? The American Consul, what a crock of shit, what did he ever come to see me for? I never knew, but I felt considerably sadder after he left, with no hope for the appeal in Hermosillo. I sat on the bed in that godforsaken cell, and I cried. The door opened while I was crying and feeling sorry for myself; it was my doctor. He told me that the blood tests showed anemia, typhoid fever, a kidney infection, a bladder infection, and he would have to check for a cyst. He exited. I sat there and cried, not from fear, from loneliness and despair. No Andrew, no word from parents, and lousy health. What more could you ask for?

At six o'clock the guards changed again. I was praying that my little friend, the jolly fat guard, would show up, and he did. His hair chopped short, his mustache light and fuzzy, his bag of food, his red-and-white bandana and his small gun. The other guard, his partner, sat in the hall, this one, Francisco, as his nameplate said, pulled up his chair and in a voice typical of a small man and characteristic of many Mexicans, said, *"Buenos noches, Susana."* I started to laugh, his nasal flat-toned voice was so serious, he sat his little self down and pulled out a comic book, his chair directly in front of my cell. He started to read it and lit a cigarette, his short, pudgy, oh-so-clean fingers tapped the ashes onto the floor where he tried to step on them with his foot, but was unable to reach them. I pretended not to see this. For lack of anything else to do, I turned on the radio. Apparently it was the Spanish-English hour when they taught Spanish to Americans. I turned up the volume, hoping I would learn a word or two. The illness and drastic change in my living style had stopped my self-taught Spanish lessons. Francisco sat outside the cell door and smoked. The teacher spoke Spanish, too quickly for me; the English was also rapid. I sat quietly and heard the voice intonation. *"Buenos noches, señors y señoritas."* Then the stock reply, *"Buenos noches."* As Mickey Mouse as this sounded, you never know what you can learn. However, the lessons had been in progress for several weeks and were far beyond "How are you?" They were talking about the sun, I thought. I tried to answer, but couldn't keep up. Francisco started to laugh, I was getting angry. I wondered how far *he'd* get in English. Then they mentioned a word that really stumped me, I mean *el sol* is enough like sun to make sense. The word I couldn't get was *árbol.* I pronounced it with the reader, *"árbol."* I had the voice intonation right on, Francisco had put down his comic book and was acting interested. I repeated *"árbol,"* but it made no sense to me. Suddenly Francisco dropped his comic book and ran into the hall. He came flying back on his little stumpy legs carrying another comic book, his little hands flipped through the pages, his face was bright red, his breath was short, "Susana, Susana," he called me to the cell door. I didn't move, what could he want? He called me again and I slipped off the bed over to the door. He was wildly pointing to a children's illustration in the comic book. It was a black-trunked, green-leaved tree. So what? I thought. He kept repeating, *"árbol, Susana, árbol."* He was so excited that I started to laugh. And then it hit me, the dear small man was trying to teach me Spanish, the way he knew best, through comic books. *Árbol* meant tree, and he was showing me a tree. I looked at him and said, *"Árbol,"* and he laughed and we both laughed and as the words came over the radio he would flip through the comic books and point out the objects to me, *árbol,* tree, *sol,* sun, *estrella,* star, and all the time his square hands pointing, gesticulating. Finally, the lesson was over and I had learned infinitely more than three words. I had learned that when someone cares it doesn't matter what the situation is. Francisco was proud and happy, I was humble and a little tearful. He was a man, short of stature, but definitely not short on compassion. I said the word friend, *"amigo,"* and he smiled and I saw him wipe a tear from his eye. I felt so guilty for a minute, this man, this good man, would also help me if he thought that I was guilty, and then I realized that he would help me no matter what. We didn't get much of a chance to rejoice; down the hall came Dr. Cardoza, running. Francisco made like a hummingbird and quickly put his comic books in his food bag and stood up. Dr. Cardoza spoke to Francisco rapidly in Spanish and Francisco opened the cell. Dr. Cardoza told me to hurry with Francisco, my parents were on the phone in the office. My heart started to beat so quickly I couldn't stand it.

Francisco grabbed my hand and half-pulled me up the hallway to the office. When I picked up the phone all I could hear was static, intense static. The offices of the hospital had air conditioning. I hadn't felt such cool air since I had been at the ocean. Francisco was standing outside the office alternately wiping his forehead with his red-and-white bandanna and checking the halls for possible threats. Where were my parents? Suddenly I heard, "Susan, it's Mommy—can you hear me?" I barely could. "Honey, we know how sick you are, Ernesto called Manuel in Mexico and he called us, we don't know if this line is O.K. or what, but try to stay in the hospital for as long as possible. We are coming down in a few days, stay there, act sick. Apparently she really didn't understand typhoid fever. "We are bringing a new lawyer. Has Gonzales been to see you yet?" "Hello, Daddy." "Hello, Susan." My mother again. "Listen, Susan, Gonzales is no good, we are coming with a new lawyer from Manuel, stay away from Andrew, don't write him or anything, do you understand? Ernesto told Manuel you still write to him," (that slimy bastard), "so stay away, this new lawyer thinks it's bad for you.

We'll explain everything when we see you, Susan." Click, she was gone. I was speechless and thoughtless. How could I not write to Andrew? I would be totally alone, I loved him. I felt absolutely desolate. Francisco noticed and tried to smile as he walked me back to the cell. But nothing worked. I felt very hot and my heart beat very quickly. I collapsed on the bed. Francisco faded away as the nurse came to give me medicine. This time a new nurse came with Connie. She seemed older and had on a pin, she was an honest to goodness registered nurse. She was going to give me a shot. I turned over on my side and she injected me. I fell asleep and dreamed of Andrew. He was behind bars and I was trying to pull him out; he couldn't get through. He was so thin, his arm was so long. I was slipping away. I must have slept all the next day and evening. I remember Salvatore cleaning my room. Mr. Castro, the friend of Manuel's, appeared mysteriously and brought me ice cream. I slept on. The next day, or the day after the day of the phone call, I got a piece of cake from Andrew, via Francisco and Adolfo, who delivered it to me. It was the banana cake with chocolate icing that I had ordered from the prisoner's father. The note told me that the party of June 18, for Andrew's birthday, was a huge success. He loved the chain and the cake and most of all he loved me. I felt sick. How would I tell him that I couldn't write to him any more? I ate the cake and tasted jail in my mouth.

If everything my parents told me was true, the judge was highly suspicious because I still communicated with Andrew. He thought, they all thought, that I, as an innocent female victim, functioning in a male-chauvinist society, should be outraged that my lover, protector, man, had endangered me. So I would have to play their game to get sympathy. I wrote him, with perhaps not guilt, but with inner visions of all the intricacies of this game I had to play. I was sure the note would be intercepted by the *comandante* and read to the D.P. and the judge. I still had confidence that Andrew would understand any innuendo. I wrote to him that he had betrayed me, on his birthday, and that I no longer loved him. I played right into everyone's hands. I felt like all choice had vanished from my life. I wrote that I knew that he understood my motives and reasons, changeable as the season, subject to the law, gafahhhh, no Mexican would understand "gafahhhh," and subtly I interplayed the words, English Literature major I, and let him know that everyone thought that I was guilty because of association, and I knew that he who was true would understand. Suddenly I saw the position he was in and the burden he would have to bear, and I wanted to say: Listen, I'll stick with you today, but I had to cover my own ass, as usual, human nature, human predicament. I was only a human being and would never, to the best of my ability, never, in my new position, hurt him. I signed the letter with a rose drawing that he would know meant that my heart was with him.

I finished the note and wondered who would deliver it. I didn't have to worry about that too long. At my cell door was Gonzales, escorted by Francisco. He hadn't seen me in over a week. He stepped in with a huge, slimy smile on his face and with his well-manicured nails and newly capped teeth. I waited for his fangs to appear. He sat down beside me and said, "Ah, poor Susana, so sick. I bring you word that Andrew and Ted are fine. You can come to visit Andrew when you are better." In my mind I wondered why he would tell me that when he knew that it would jeopardize my chances of being believed. Some lawyer. He pulled at his pants and continued. "All goes well, I promise you be out" (yeah, like he told me we would only be there 72 hours) "and I have very good connections in Hermosillo for appeals. I am a very important man. Now, I need more money from your father to go to Hermosillo, when he come down?" "I think soon," I said. "Well, Susana," he was picking his caps now, "you need nothing?" His voice lowered and he said, with Francisco straining to hear every word, "I smart man. I know you head of the group. Mafia lady. No problem, I help you." I wanted to punch him in the mouth, trying in his insidious little way to ingratiate himself. Self-restraint, Susan, practice a little. All I said, with steam pouring out of my mouth and ears, was, "I don't want to see Andrew any more. He is bad. You give him this note." "Yes, he is very bad," he agreed. "But you still love him." I said, "No, man, and thanks." He exited, stage right, the note firmly planted in his sweaty palm. I knew he would deliver it to the *coman-*

dante, personally. He's a sneak, like the rest of us. I knew that he would take money and pretend to do good. He didn't even try to protect me. A new lawyer was necessary.

All this mental exertion and I was getting dazed again. The guards changed again, my dinner came, I gave it to the guards. My shot came, I took it in the other hip. I fell asleep. When I woke up I was sweating profusely and the lights were in the hallway. I went to the bathroom and threw up. The two guards were talking rapidly, and I looked again and saw that there were four *Federales* in the hallway, armed with rifles. They were coming closer, what was going on? Were they going to shoot me? What the fuck, everything had become so bizarre, things had gone too far. Instead, two of them sat themselves outside my cell in the hallway and glared at me. What were they doing here? Now there were six people guarding me. I cursed in my limited Spanish and resolved to study more. I wondered if I should move. I prayed for an answer. Instead, I wrote a note to the *comandante* asking what the fuck was going on. Did he think I was trying to escape or what? I gave it to one of the *Federales,* knowing full well that Ernesto would translate it. The whole setup was getting too melodramatic for me. I dozed off and when I awoke Dr. Cardoza was there, in the early morning light, and I asked him what was going on. He said that all he knew was that the newspapers had carried an article that very morning stating that I was trying to escape, that I was head of the ring. I knew in my heart that Gonzales had started that rumor, Dr. Cardoza had told me that Gonzales worked for the newspaper. I was furious, big deal, what could I do? The guards paced back and forth in the hallway.

For the next few days I ate less and less. I got no reply from Andrew, my blood pressure, which they took twice a day, went up to 190. At night, armed *Federales* watched me like hawks. I spit at everyone. How could they think that I was trying to escape? Still no word from the *comandante.* I was dazed and confused, I had fever, I laughed only with Francisco. I learned the words for fear and court and mother and father and guns. The newspapers carried articles everyday about my supposed attempts at escape. Gonzales never reared his ugly head. I dreamt a slender thought, until past and present faded into nothing and only the slim reality of my own dream remained. And my dream became a prayer. I had to get more clear in my head and understand my motives and the position I was in of dependence on everyone and belief in no one. I had to take care of myself, because this way brings problems, I cannot run from place to place in search of the Holy Grail. I only pray that I am not too late.

*O*nly Francisco brought light to me. He spoke of marijuana and told me that he got high. He assured me that my parents would rescue me. The doctors told me that I was run down and couldn't go back to the jail. Gonzales never showed. July would be here soon. Manuel called me from Mexico City, my parents would be down the next day. And so I had been in the hospital for one week and in prison for over a month. My doctor told me how sick I was. He made jokes that I had enough diseases for the whole hospital. For the first time in my life I was too thin. I couldn't gain weight and the doctor was worried about my anemia. So twice a day for fifteen days, they gave me shots of vitamins. The student nurses were not very good shot givers, having had very little experience. Connie would ease down the hall with a tin tray in her fat hands. My needle for the shot would be exposed to all the bacteria of the air, plus the dirt on the tray. I tried to tell her about my hygienic opinions, but she would have none of them. When she arrived at my cell the attending guard would unlock the door and step into the hallway, for protocol's sake. Then Connie would turn me over on my side, pull up my little hospital dress and jab this huge needle into my hip. I tried to show her and the other girls who came to the cell at six o'clock in the morning how to inject me properly, but no one listened. So I endured the pain and watched my hips turn black with bruise marks.

Salvatore was another privileged character for whom the guards would open the cells. Every morning at around ten o'clock he would slide down the hall with his buckets and mops. His sky blue jacket was always immaculate, his smile always wide. Every morning it was *"Buenos dias, Susana."* I played the radio while he cleaned and whistled. He was so meticulous in his cleaning, very humble. All the guards made fun of him, especially Francisco, who took his painful awkwardness as love for me. Simultaneously, the nurses would come to change the sheets and bring me a clean hospital gown. Somehow, unbeknownst to me, I had developed a friend in the laundry room. Instead of a long and fairly unflattering gown, I was always sent a little hospital minidress. It was no big thing really, but it was a nice gesture. Periodically, Dr. Cardoza would visit with a magazine and conversation about Jaime, my long-lost friend from jail. I wrote Jaime one note to tell him not to be afraid, it had pictures of rainbows and butterflies on it. Dr. Cardoza clipped articles out of magazines, and I did likewise. Mine were about the harmful side effects of shock therapy, his were pro-shock treatment articles. So our debate continued. I worried about Andrew and if he had understood my note, apparently the *comandante* had understood the epistle and had, as I had suspected, told everyone that I was through with Andrew. At least all the guards knew about it and they mainly made up my world. I tried to get permission for Ernesto to visit my cell, to get him to deliver messages to Andrew, but it was better that I didn't get that opportunity, as he could not be trusted.

The days were endlessly hot and oppressively humid and silent. My only real respite from daily solitude were the cleaners, nurses, and guards. Sometimes, I really felt as if I was losing my mind, dressed in white, in a white cell, with white heat and vacant spaces in my days filled only by white-hot reflections of the sun. There was really no one to talk to. I couldn't trust anyone, everyone was too concerned about being recognized and appreciated for turning me in had I done anything wrong. I paced back and forth in my cell; my blood pressure was very high. I felt so lonely, and yet in some way, complete. I was confused. I couldn't have told Andrew that I had grown to resent him for the part of myself that was weak and sneaky.

At night, armed *Federales* guarded me either to keep someone out or to make sure that I stayed in; so far, I had no real idea why they were there. And all the time the newspapers featured articles about my attempted escape, the planned escape the *gringita* had arranged. Dr. Cardoza would suggest occasionally that Gonzales was writing the articles, but when I pressed him, he would say that it was only gossip. My typhoid fever was getting better, although occasionally I would lapse into fevers of 103. But generally, I felt less like I was living in a soundproof bubble of fever.

Many things were changing. I was becoming increasingly friendly with my guards. I told them all my parents were coming soon. The evening Manuel called to tell me my parents would be there two things happened. I got a telegram from my folks saying that they would not be there for two days. As usual everything in Mexico was confused. Then new orders from the *comandante* came saying that instead of two guards on duty with me every twelve hours, there would only be one guard. They were getting more lenient with me in some ways. I hoped that, out of every pair of guards, the one friendlier to me would stay. That afternoon, Alberto Leyva came to guard me by himself. We had become friendlier with each other, he had apologized for that "romantic" evening when he had tried to coerce me into sex with him and Juanita. As my Spanish improved, with help from him and Francisco and Thomas, the other guard, I began to understand more of his personality. He tried to explain to me in simple Spanish that every day was the same to him, the dull police work with no money and no hope for improvement. There was no money for clothes or extra food. There was no hope for his children's futures. Slowly, I began to understand the despair of these poor people who lived slowly, and in fear of speaking the truth about their government. These conversations took tedious hours, infinite patience, and ultimate interest in each other as human beings. In his beige uniform with his thick black hair and deep eyes, he would try to explain life in Mexico, the heat and depression, the boredom. He also told me of his wife and two children, his sickness of tortillas, his drinking bouts to relieve the boredom. I tried, in Spanish, without verb tenses, to ask him why he didn't try to improve his lot in life, why he didn't get a job working at a hotel as a waiter; the pay was better, the opportunity greater, and the tourists would surely relieve boredom. Alberto would consider the ideas and then find a reason not to make a move. He was afraid to fail. Man makes his own fate, Alberto.

Then, one day after one of our talks he excused himself for a few minutes and then came back. He said that he had made a call and all he had to do to qualify for a job at a hotel was to learn English, would I help? I wanted to laugh, but sat down with my trusty dictionary and made a list of all the words I knew in Spanish, plus words used often in hotels. Then I put the English equivalents next to the Spanish words, folded the paper down the center, and made a game out of guessing the correct translations of the Spanish words. But then I had to take the English and write it phonetically in Spanish so that he could understand the alien pronunciations. Alberto was ecstatic; we must have talked for the whole twelve hours he was there, and I thanked God for this man, plus Francisco and Thomas, who took my mind off myself. Alberto would beam as I asked him *"mañana,"* in Spanish and his answer in English was a halting "to-mar-ah." He especially liked "I love you." So, having reached this degree of intimacy and shared loneliness with Alberto I tried to ask him why I needed two *Federales* with machine guns at night to guard me. Suddenly our communication ended, he didn't understand me. No, Susana, he didn't know and good-by. Finally, after I had gotten furious, he told me, as far as I could understand, that he really didn't know. He was merely a lowly policeman, no one told him anything. Six o'clock came, Alberto left with his list, and down the hall, proud as a peacock, with hair shiny, little gun polished, and uniform immaculate, pranced Francisco. He was so funny this time that I laughed at him. He took out his little red-and-white bandanna and wiped his forehead, *"Mucho calor,"* meaning, "Very hot." He repeated this several times. I agreed. Then he sat himself directly in front of the cell, pulled out a cigarette, lit one, and asked me how I felt. He was the first person who had asked me that in a long time. I explained to Francisco, who either out of sympathy or real knowledge of English, understood my Spanish better than anyone else, how alone I felt, how nervous I was about seeing my parents, how very confused I was. I wanted to tell him I missed Andrew, but I was afraid that he would repeat it to the *comandante*. I wanted to trust him, but couldn't. However, he asked me if I missed Andrew and I nodded my head. The day had been intense for me, with no siesta because of Alberto, so after eating a dinner of banana and grapefruit juice, I fell asleep.

When I woke there were two small girls in bare feet and pony tails bringing Francisco his dinner. They were his adorable little daughters, look-alike little cherubs in their faded dresses smelling of Clorox. He introduced them to me, I shook hands through the bars, and they giggled the universal giggle of little girls. He gave them each one centavo, equivalent to one-twelfth of a dollar, and they ran down the hall. Francisco politely offered me some of his food, cold tortilla with meat and hot pepper sauce. I refused, politely; I wasn't quite ready. I asked Francisco how many children he had, he told me nine, then said maybe ten or thirteen, he wasn't sure, and we laughed. The nurse came to give me my shot, Francisco opened the cell for her and slipped down the hallway. When he returned, we turned on the radio to listen to the English lesson.

Tonight the lesson was about planting a garden, just what I needed to know in my position. Little Francisco jumped out of the chair and pretended to dig in the ground for seeds, then he tried to imitate a flower blooming, the sun setting. I laughed until I cried. Finally my doctor came, took my temperature, which was high, gave me medication and asked if I was having trouble sleeping. When I said yes, he ordered sleeping pills for me. I took one, said good night to Francisco and slept soundly. When I awoke Thomas was there. He was perhaps the sternest of my three favorite guards. However, he was kind to me, just quiet, and not interested in humor or personal discussions. He later taught me about cards. We were sitting there, me in a clean hospital gown, sweating and staring into space, Thomas on his straight-back chair, when I heard three or four sets of footsteps coming down the hallway. I heard a whistle, the traditional Nadler-family whistle that my father always gave when he came home and we children gave at various times, and I knew at that moment that my parents had arrived. I thought that probably they had brought Manuel with them, and the new lawyer. It was July 4, Independence Day, and, I hoped, a good sign. Thomas stood up very straight and around the corner stepped my parents.

My mother looked Spanish, beautiful and tearful, dressed in black. My father looked tired, his Brooks Brothers pink shirt was the hottest color I had seen since I had been in the hospital. He was stately and looked as if he was holding my mother up. Behind them walked two men, one of whom was Manuel, my savior, hero Mexican godfather. The other was a short, heavy-set man; he later billed himself as a little Marlon Brando. All this, these individual pictures, flashed before my eyes like olden-day moving pictures, one shot at a time, only I was one reel behind and not reacting to the picture at hand, rather the picture of five minutes ago. Thomas became quite nervous and would not allow anyone in my cell, after all, he was under orders, I was in solitary confinement, this meant no visitors, he couldn't know these people were my parents and lawyers. I was still thought of as trying to make an escape. I tried to explain to Thomas that he must trust me as a friend. Usually emotion works when all else fails. Thomas looked at Manuel, very fair-haired and light-skinned, dressed in a seersucker summer suit. Thomas thought that Manuel was my father. He motioned that Manuel and my mother should go in and Manuel started to laugh quickly and in Spanish he explained who he was, who the little Marlon Brando was, my lawyer, and introduced my father. He explained his presence as being a friend of the family's, and the interpreter for the lawyer. As long as I was in trouble, from the first moment I met him until the last day I saw him, I realized that Manuel was a very special person. He, on the word of one of my father's friends, left his home, and never accepting a cent from my family except to cover his expenses, devoted himself to the cause of my freedom. He is very rare among men. He is, incidentally, an idealist who believed, not really in my innocence, but the innocence of my family. He believed that people of my parent's stature and integrity needn't suffer for the inexcusable mistake of their daughter.

Often I wondered what happens to all the American kids, out to make a fast buck, have a good time, and beat the law, what happens to those of them who are busted overseas and whose parents have no money to afford the best criminal lawyers in the country, who cannot fly down and stay at their children's sides and see the judge and pay off the chemists so the analysis goes faster, and talk the good doctors into keeping their children in the hospitals and leave their homes and families for extended periods and impress the natives as honorable people whose children didn't stray too far. Because when you are busted overseas and guilty until proven innocent, and have no money or influence, you are finished. There is no hope and hope is the most important thing one can possess. When hope goes, it is as if the heart dies. It was difficult enough to be busted and thrown around and be sick and confined and scared shitless, without having to face the ultimate possibility of a long sentence. At this moment I had very little hope of avoiding a twenty-seven-year sentence, but somehow, somewhere, I always felt, well, maybe my parents can save me. Basically, one can never accept a fate that is thrust upon one, especially a fate that admits no freedom or real life. When I thought of spending twenty-seven years in jail, I could not believe that I would ever get out, but I also could not accept that I, Susan Beth Nadler, life-lover, intellectual, would have this particular karma. This is why in life my actions reflected no fear. Not only did I use drugs to bend my perspectives to my own liking when I thought I was protected, I never really had to stop and think in my life because my parents had made all the decisions for me. They had chosen my schools, my clothes, my tastes, my friends, I was not even capable of choosing a man without subconsciously looking to them for approval. More than anything else I knew that they had raised me in their particular way out of love, never intending to hurt me, and more than anything else I can say now, teach your children, but make them, if possible, responsible for all their own actions, so that some day they don't end up smuggling drugs because someone tells them all the time that it will be all right, they can't get caught. I was so surprised at these unprepared-for thoughts that flooded my mind for the first time that hot morning when I saw my mother's tears and my father's restraint. I was so vulnerable at this point, so beaten, that I would listen to anything they told me. But for some reason I was getting more clear in my head, and I thought what I thought. For the first time in my life I saw my parents as two people who had tried their very best to do what was right for me, and in trying so hard had omitted to let me choose what was right and what was wrong. Yet I also realized in this unbelievable situation of immobility and desperation, that I would again be dependent on them to save me. Oh, rescue me!

Where would that put me, depending on someone else to extricate me from trouble? Everyone was talking all at once I realized, as I tried to get caught up in the present reel. My mother was thrusting upon me Elizabeth Arden creams that she had given me my whole life, telling me that I must take care of my skin at all times; better she should have told me to take care of my ass. She was also handing me a bra, of all things, good-by Band-Aided nipples.

The next two hours are indelibly impressed on my mind as the most intense hours I had gone through since the bust. I was introduced, via Manuel, to my new attorney, his personal friend and the best criminal lawyer in Mexico City. I asked him, Señor Icaza, what sign he was, he looked slightly surprised, this ruggedly handsome, obvious male chauvinist, and in broken English, he answered, "Aries, Aries, like you Susan, wild, crazy, and now, we work." He then proceeded to explain to me that Gonzales was a terribly (sic) lawyer and that he, Joe Icaza, would put in a petition with the judge for a retrial in La Paz. Gonzales had said that this was impossible. Nothing was impossible for Joe. He then handed me a huge sheaf of papers that turned out to be the transcripts of my interrogation by the D.P. translated into English. Here, as Joe (he insisted that I call him Joe) raced through with me, were the four charges against me: 1.) possession; 2.) importation; 3.) transportation; and 4.) acquisition. These brought my maximum sentence to twenty-seven years. He told me that he wanted to make sure that I understood that he wanted to get me out legally, not by tricks, so that I would never feel strange about getting out. I guess that he was really talking about his own conscience, since he was very antidrug. He was talking as quickly as any American and I was starting to talk as slowly as any Mexican. He would prove in court, 1.) That I couldn't be guilty of possession because the package was not in my name and the hash was not visible to the naked eye before the armoire was broken into; 2.) that I was not guilty of importation because the package was not imported by me, no arrangements were made by me or in my name; 3.) that I had not driven the truck that carried the armoire to my apartment (here he needed witnesses, the police who had been watching us) and I had not helped to carry the package up the stairs to my apartment; and 4.) I had not personally acquired the hash, and here he needed the Aero Cargo boy who had delivered the telegram to testify that I had not received the telegram.

This over, Joe puffed; he was very sharp and intense, his beady eyes tried to penetrate into my essence. I locked him out. I was his client, he would never know the real truth. He was reassembling all his papers now to go to the judge and ask for a retrial. On the way he would stop and talk to my doctor to ask him to keep me as long as possible in the hospital. And did I understand that I was not to communicate with Andrew at all, Susan? It was not good. Joe wanted my parents to come now, his way of stating things was always so confusing. "I want me go," meant he wanted them to go, and I want you go meant he wanted to go. So he wanted everyone to go so that he could talk to the judge and take my family and let the judge see that I was not from a Mafia family. Later, it turned out that the judge never really believed my parents were really my parents; he thought that I was too criminal-like to have such good people for family. Everyone ran out, Joe and my parents to the judge's chambers, and Manuel to the hotel to make sure everything was all right. My parents' hurried comment before they left was that I was extraordinarily thin (no kidding, ma, I had typhoid fever), and that they would bring me dinner. Good-by and good luck. I felt like standing up and saluting when they left—honest to God, a very strange reaction to have.

That day began a two-week period of craziness in which I became more detached and more removed from the details of the situation. I stepped out of myself, so to speak, and saw myself as a product of the stupendous sixties, a wealthy background, a spoiled family, and myself a drug-confused woman who was coming down, along with her family, from a six-year high, where truth was a long-lost friend, and unreality was maintained so that no one would get hurt. For example, stoned out of my mind in L.A., I can remember calling my parents to tell them hello and never even coming close to the issue of how are you really, because really they always knew but didn't want to be confronted with the truth; it hurt them. And so it goes, and so there I was, busted in La Paz, forgetting my real being, and just starting to realize where and who I was. I was alone, surrounded with honest, good people trying to get me out of jail, and I was guilty. But if I was guilty I deserved to stay in jail, didn't I? And if I was guilty and the people were so good and honest, why were they trying to get me out? My conception of justice was obviously not right on, but what were all the good and honest people trying to do, convince themselves that I was not guilty, or did they know that I was guilty and not care? Or was jail not really a universal punishment, but just for the poor? Were the rich exempt from guilt? Did the good, honest people think that integrity was in having laws, but that any way of sneaking out of them was all right?

That evening about 7:15 my parents returned with Joe and Manuel. On duty was Alberto, very excited because he had studied his English and was prepared to try to converse with my parents. Already the news had spread through the town that my parents had arrived. This fact greatly impressed the Mexicans who were so family-conscious. They felt that perhaps I was not so bad after all if my parents were coming to see me. And such wealth! Alberto told me that all the police were sorry that they didn't work at the hospital, as if by magic my parents' money would rub off on them and turn their pesos into gold. My assemblage arrived with a full-course meal from the hotel where they were staying. It included steak, salad, grilled vegetables, bread, fruit, and cake. I wasn't sure if I could eat, but I would give it a good try. While I was eating my lawyer told me it was almost certain, as certain as anything was in Mexico, that my retrial would be in three days. I stopped eating; I couldn't believe that I was getting a retrial. Hope began to surge through my veins again. Secondarily, and more painfully, was the awareness that I would see Andrew again at the trial, the pain of my lost love beckoned me. I rejected it, I couldn't handle the pain now. My father, so shiny and clean in white, told me that they had seen the judge that day. He had not believed at first that they were my parents; however, they finally convinced him. It had been a profitable day. Then my lawyer pulled his coup—from his brief case he took a portfolio of letters, gathered by my parents at the exclusive wishes of Joe, to be used in just this case. The letters were letters of recommendation as to my character. The food stuck in my throat. There were letters from my Sunday school teachers saying that I was a good girl, letters from high school teachers attesting to my honesty and intelligence, letters from rabbis, the chief of police, supreme court judges, outstanding citizens, all to be used as character references by my lawyer, and painfully solicited by my father to save his daughter. I looked my father in his eyes and cried as he looked at me and I looked at him and I knew what he had been through. Every letter had been carried personally to the Mexican consulate in Philadelphia and translated into Spanish, signed, sealed, and sent to the American Embassy in Mexico City, where they were verified, attested to, stamped, and approved. The hours and the dedication. . . . Next, Joe pulled out a very strange letter. It was also signed, stamped, sealed, translated, and approved by the Philadelphia consulate and the American Embassy in Mexico City, but it had originated in L.A. I remembered. . . . One of the charges the judge was unfavorably impressed with was my possession of tiny "hash" tablets he had had analyzed in the local laboratories. These pills were actually Innerclean, an herbal laxative for neurotic health-food freaks like me. My father had called the president of this company, a man eighty years of age and Jewish, and explained the situation to him. He had been most sympathetic and had written a letter to the judge, in care of my father, exactly stating the content of each pill, chemically broken down by percentage. Meanwhile, the pills had been sent to Mexico City laboratories where they were again being analyzed. Five hundred dollars for air fare for Manuel and Joe, hotel rooms, copies of documents, phone calls to Mexico, doctors' bills for me, phone calls to me, fees to Gonzales, fees to Joe.

My father explained to me that evening that the reason Gonzales was not dropped from the case was because Mexico was slow and corrupt on many levels and neither Manuel nor Joe would ever know if Gonzales would tell the judge untrue things about me. So they had to humor him to the tune of $4000 and pay for his lunches with Joe and his supposed dinners with the judge's clerk. You are at an obvious disadvantage in a foreign country, you never really know what is going on. My circuits were overloaded with information and guilt, great guilt over my parents, who deep down inside knew that I was guilty, but had to ask people for help as if I weren't.

I was overloaded with food. I hadn't really eaten in over a month. My parents would stay until the retrial, they would have much time to talk to me, if they could handle it, and so for the second time that day everyone busily prepared to go. My mother, hands shaking, reapplied her lipstick, my father tucked in his shirt, Joe packed up his brief case. Manuel talked to Alberto and no one looked me in the eyes. Manuel suddenly burst into laughter that echoed the length of the corridor, shook the thick night, and bounced off the stars. "My God, Susan, so you have been teaching the guards English and they teach you Spanish. Soon you will speak like a low-class Mexican." And all the adults laughed and I said, "These low-class Mexicans, they look me in the eyes and feel my heart and they are solid, like earth, they give. They care, they teach me, they are good. They care about my spirit. I thank them." No one spoke, but suddenly Alberto interrupted the silence, proudly, with his newly learned English; he raised his eyes toward me and stated very clearly, "I lub you."

16

*M*aya, had my life so far been nothing but maya, nothing but flowing fantasies, longing for things that are unreal and yet are my life? Am I able to be an ascetic? I seriously doubt it—I want to be free, tomorrow I will have been in jail for six weeks, *bastante tiempo*—I don't know, sometimes I think that when I'm free I'll go to Los Angeles and stay and write my music. I owe my parents a lot, but is it worth my happiness? I am too old to be told what to do.

The days passed on, becoming hotter and hotter. I spent my time laughing with Alberto and Francisco about the minutiae of life and having very heavy discussions with my parents about the ethics of living. My mother was really too incoherent at this point to make sense, she only wanted to know if I felt they had made a mistake with me while I was growing up. However, these talks were long since overdue, I didn't want to waste our energies on discussions of the past, which barely lasts. I had a hard time explaining to my father that I had invested money in the hash deal, that I had not been afraid of being caught, that the law had meant nothing to me. They didn't understand my head, how I had laughed at it all as a big joke, good, evil, right, wrong. Where are the absolutes? Because deep down inside I was starting to wonder what I was really learning from the whole situation. I was learning personally that a change was necessary in my life, because I could no longer just go with the flow. I had to have some purpose in my existence, some meaning to myself so that I didn't place myself in situations that jeopardized my own life. I had to learn or at least learn to discern between right and discipline, and wrong and easy. But if I got out of jail, so quickly, what would I really learn? I lied to the D.P., to my lawyers, to the judge, to my parents. The only people I didn't lie to were Alberto and Francisco because they weren't interested in whether I was guilty or not. They were interested in me as a human being who cared for them and could laugh, learn, and teach them. So I lied, to cover my guilt. And yet, what was a worse lie?

A lie is a lie is a lie is a lie is a lie is it not? To have people obtain my freedom, which I so greatly desired but didn't deserve because I was guilty and they knew it? Wasn't that more craziness? Wasn't it another example of how I got out of everything with minimum suffering, and a call to Daddy. What was I to learn from all this—that to smuggle hash is bad because it is against the law, but to lie to the law to get the smuggler out is all right? I didn't want to stay in jail, yet deep down inside, I knew somehow that I would never amend my ways, only rechannel them, if I got out so easily. But God, don't listen to this foolishness, help me to get out, I will change, I promise, despite the fact that I will get out like I got in, shakily. How can I ever be responsible for my own actions when someone else has become responsible for me? And my morning song, my pretrial guilt was interrupted by my good father and mother with breakfast on a tray for their daughter and a roll for Francisco, their little friend, and forced love and smiles for the child who was destroying their lives. Close on their heels, and unbeknownst to them, guarded by four *Federales,* came the *comandante.* He surprised us all so much when he entered that there was absolute silence. Francisco saluted and stood at attention, my mother looked at me as if to ask who the man was, my father was restrained. The *comandante* rapidly checked out the room, walked to the porch, re-entered in his immaculate gray outfit and pistols. I had forgotten or put out of mind the *comandante* and his Wild West routine, I had slightly forgotten jail, because reality is the present. That is why time is so unimportant to the Mexicans; they do not rush the future, which they know they cannot control, they live in the moment they are in and enjoy

it. The *comandante* had not rushed to answer my note, he waited for
an appropriate moment when it would be most dramatic. And this
clever man, with his bodyguards and heavy aura of violence, he
knew what he was doing. He paused dramatically and said to my
parents, "You want Susan dead or alive?" Jesus, man, he had
watched too many "Gunsmoke" reruns, my father looked at my
mother and she looked alarmedly at him and they looked at me and
the *comandante* said, "If you want her alive, then she must go back
to jail," and my mother started to cry and the *comandante* looked
away and from his pocket pulled my note to him where I had asked
him why he needed armed guards and said, "Someone, Mafia, call
hospital, say going to kill Susan, need *Federales* here, her not safe."
And my father tried to answer him by saying it was out of the question that I go back to the jail, and I wasn't from the Mafia and there
must be some mistake. Such melodrama! That goddam *comandante*
wanted me in jail so he wouldn't have to spare any guards at the
hospital. Joe, my lawyer, had talked to the good doctor and I knew
I would never have to leave the hospital, at least not for a while.
The good doctor had totally understood about my good parents and
everything would be all right. Nice try at the Wild West, *comandante,* I thought, nice try and good-by. He made several attempts to
explain to my father the danger I was in. I finally understood that
with so little to do and such energy, the *comandante* liked a little
melodrama. The only thing that I could figure out that had happened was that some American called up to ask where I was, probably a tourist, and the *comandante,* ready for the worst, assumed that
somebody wanted to kill me. He left in a puff of smoke. At least
now I understood why the *Federales* guarded me at night, not that it
made a difference. I understood, my parents were upset, and Francisco's wondrous brown eyes stood open like gates. The situation
was becoming increasingly difficult to take. How could I respect
anyone? The *comandante* probably was lying or exaggerating; we
would never know. My parents would like to get me out, and I was
being tried for smuggling and lying. The humor of it all faded fast,
brother, the girl who had been able to laugh at it all was being replaced by a woman confused as to the meaning of integrity.

My parents left to go back to the hotel to prepare for the retrial and I was sort of surprised by another visit from the *comandante,* who came to talk. Jesus, I don't see or hear from the man, despite my requests, for a month, then here he is two times in one day. He came to apologize to me for the SS-type tactics and told me he had been overwrought that day. Big shit, like that explained it all. We talked though, and I felt like a total fake and sham, the only way to impress him was to pretend innocence. Does this man really believe that I didn't know about the hash? This man is very bizarre. He saw *Steppenwolf* on my bed and told me that he had read it too. Then we discussed the choices man has to make and good and evil. It was very strange to discuss such things with this man, who to me represented a sheriff, and yet his intelligence was evident. What a complex life he leads. He is sensitive but tells me, "Susana, must have respect from my men—they think sensitivity is what you call for the women, and understand only *machismo.* I try, many times I want to cry, I must to live a lie." And I came to understand that many people accept lying as a way of life. He looked at me many times and said, "Why someone want to kill you Susana, you Mafia?" And I knew that no matter how close I felt to him, I could never be honest. He left, I felt bereft of another illusion, gone, poof, the *comandante* lived two lives. Later he sent men to take me to my retrial.

The retrial was outrageous and regular, as retrials go. The good doctor brought me a valium to stop my hands from shaking, my mother brought me a dress to make me pretty; the phony letters spoke for themselves. The fan spun around slowly, ineffectually. I couldn't believe that I was in court again, only this time my parents were there to watch me. I felt like I was under a microscope, would I ever get out? I wanted to yell that I was guilty, and get it over with, but I couldn't. Then I saw Andrew and I knew how he felt, he would never be able to get out, his parents didn't have any money. Andrew looked at me longingly; but my lawyer hit me in the arm if I ever dared look his way. My parents felt sorry for Ted, the real culprit, although at this point who was I to judge guilt? Joe and I had gone over the questions that were likely to come up in the morning. The judge was not even there. The fat woman typed her ass off, and the interpreter was Ernesto, who assured me secretly that he understood my position. The points in my favor were made one by one. The Aero Cargo boy testified that I never had jumped up and down and kissed Andrew when he delivered the telegram, like he had testified the first time. Of course he was lying too. My parents had talked to him the night before. There was a letter from my doctor saying that I was, in all probability, ill with typhoid fever the day the package was delivered, so I had not been trying to leave the country to go back to L.A. and make connections, only to see a doctor. I never knew if I had had typhoid fever or not, but at this point I knew that everyone was lying. The *Federales* all testified one by one that I had never touched the armoire and I nodded, my head on my shoulder, from the heat and the valium. Everyone smiled at me reassuringly. The only real laugh of the day (overshadowed by fogs and tears) was the sermonette on Innerclean delivered by Joe, who explained about herbal laxatives to the D.P. and the Clerk of the Court. The men all giggled at this shadowy vulgarity and Ted and I swore at the whole laxative world. I tried to touch Andrew with my feelings but knew that somewhere I had really failed him because I was cooperating with my family, indirectly against him, to make myself look good. Another lie, another cry, another confusion for me, but Andrew knew the game well and blew me a kiss. I met the kiss with an embrace in the air that went nowhere. And the trial was over, my father took off his tie and my mother unclasped her pearls. The judge had forty-eight hours to decide my guilt or innocence again. Joe made it clear to him that he was my lawyer alone, and not connected with Andrew or Ted. The *Federales* drove me back to the hospital and stopped to get me, the little darlings, some ice cream.

When I returned to the hospital Francisco was waiting with a present for me, some freshly baked tortillas from his wife and two avocados. He asked me how it went and he played along as I told him how bad Andrew was, and I knew he didn't care, he only wished me free. As we ate the good food together and he wiped his forehead off with his little bandanna, he tried to tell me that my parents and their money would get me out, not to worry because money could do all. I told him the judge could not be bought, Joe had already inquired, but he shook his head and said time would heal all. The Mexican attitude toward time: go slowly, so slowly, you can't rush time anyway. If I was meant to get out, I would. And we laughed at skinny Juanita who brought me back a late lunch of beans and potatoes. Francisco flirted with her and when I asked her for two jars and some toothpicks, she looked amazed but Francisco said, *"Si, Juanita, ella está bené."* She brought them to me and I took two avocado seeds from Francisco and put water in the jars and three toothpicks in each seed, to hold them in the water. I put my little plants on the front porch, in the sun, where they would grow to be strong, like Francisco. They were going to be his, for the food and truth and friendship he gave me. He became very shy when I told him, but he grabbed my hand and held it. I took off my ring from other days, of two silver hands clasping, and gave it to him. He smiled. (Neither he nor Alberto locked me in any longer, but sat in front of my open cell, and watched me.) I went into the bathroom then and undressed, put on my hospital gown and lay in bed. Soon the vapors of sleep gathered me in and I dreamt of avocado fields with high trees covered with green fruits, and Francisco and his children walked through the fields, proud of their land and gardens. I slept well. Gone were the lies and fears, for I was beginning to accept the fate thrust upon me. Perhaps it was the only thing that would teach me.

The answer, or the judge's decision was "Guilty." Guilty still, or still guilty, or always was and would continue to be guilty to this judge in his court in La Paz. It was a huge defeat for my parents, an indication of the future to me, and only a slight delay to Joe, who was used to the Mexican courts. My hopes were starting to dwindle, maybe I would get the punishment I deserved by law and remain for twenty-seven years, but this thought clutched my falling heart that fled in fear. My parents were to leave the next day. We had a consultation with Joe that evening. His next step—he would do anything to put off a lengthy appeal in Hermosillo—was to put in a petition for my liberty. This petition would be a lengthy, terribly legal document that would demand my freedom on the basis of my innocence and the lack of evidence to prove my guilt. The petition would not involve Andrew or Ted, only me, and Joe felt sure that the judge would be swayed by his fine defense that erased all signs of guilt, my parents and their very ethical vibes, my disassociation from Andrew, who had wronged me, and the letters of character reference. A fine defense that trickily proved on technical grounds that I was not guilty, that used my parents' vibes, not mine, and that used my disassociation (which was not my idea) because we knew the judge wanted it; plus the phony letters of character reference. It was the middle of July; the petition for liberty would be answered by the middle of August, and I had about three and a half weeks to wait. Joe put his papers away and told my parents he would meet them later.

A final conversation with my parents. My mother became hysterical about leaving her child behind, she was wild, promised me the world when I was free. My father cleared his throat and told me not to worry, I had the best that money could buy. He left me some money. I wanted to say that I needed someone to rescue me from my moral dilemma. But wasn't it time I learned to rescue myself? Basically, I was afraid he would not want to support me any more, if I said this, so I told him that I appreciated all of his help and this he understood. He would order books from Mexico City from Manuel, and he had brought two with him. I looked, my poor father, he had brought with him the same two he had given me before, *The Greening of America*, and *The French Lieutenant's Woman*. I pretended that they were new.

After the hysterics of my mother and the rationality of my father there was silence. Little Francisco sat at the cell door, observing it all. Suddenly he began to speak, to break the silence or not, I never knew. I was put in the position of the interpreter. He directed most of his conversation to my father. I translate here as best I can.

"Susana, tell your father, sometimes in life a man must say he has tried as best he can, and the rest is up to God. Tell your father he has done as best as possible. Tell him that my father died never even knowing that I was to be born a man." Then Francisco stood up and extended his little chest to its fullest extent. "Tell your father that life is not always so simple. Tell your father that I have eleven, ahhh, thirteen children, and my eldest son wants to attend college. Tell your father that I can't afford it." Francisco's voice was getting shakier. "Tell your father that I feel often like a failure because I can't send my eldest son to college, or send my daughter to nursing school, or take my wife to the cinema. But tell your father that I am still a man and I know that God understands, even though I am small of stature, I am a man, too. Tell your father that children are not all of it, ah Susana, I do not know the words." And he sat in front of my father, in the heat, in his little police outfit, with the sweat dripping down his face, mopping his brow with his little red-and-white bandanna, and I saw tears flow down his cheeks. And my father's white shirt stuck to him and he had tears in his eyes as he told me to tell Francisco that he understood the troubles of life, but he too still loved getting up in the morning and breathing, but that sometimes he felt defeated, because he had tried so hard with me, and I had not understood, and then my father started to cry, and my mother started to cry, and I started to cry too. And we all fell asleep, Francisco in his little chair, my mother and I on the bed, my father on the chair. We all fell asleep in tears of heat.

That night Francisco was gone and Alberto came to replace him, with news that I was to be allowed to walk in the hospital courtyard with my guards and see the trees. Joe's plan had worked, the *comandante* had been impressed with my parents enough to trust me more. I put on my thongs, Alberto locked my cell behind me, and we walked down that long corridor. How many times I had craved the air. We stepped out the door and the cool evening air smelled like perfume, intoxicating me and making me dizzy. The courtyard was filled with trees and bushes and grass. Around it was a fence, and as we walked across the length of the yard, I saw my old apartment across the street and remembered looking out the windows so many times, stoned and eating chocolate pudding and thinking that the hospital was a mental institution. Alberto nodded at my apartment and shook his head, I looked away. We walked back into the hospital. Alberto and I were both happy in the air but I was nostalgic for other days and he was nostalgic for other days too. He told me how important it was to go outside and feel the air, he told me how hope lived in the air, in the trees, he pulled out two mangos from his dinner bag, and we sat in the hallway and ate our mangos, two friends in the night, listening to young interns, lonely, down the hall, serenade the moon with love songs. Life was as sweet as the mango that night. I had a friend, I was at home. All felt right. If only I could tell the truth and be free, but that wasn't what was meant for me, and I started to feel desperation again and my friend Alberto knew it too. I walked into my cell and wondered how I could pretend that I was changing, and still lie.

*T*he green earth, the green wind, illuminated light. The hospital courtyard, the failing banana plants. I am in my white hospital gown, like a spirit, so imbued with this Spanish literature. There are so many things I want to say this golden breezy evening—where all looks fairy-like, like an image from the movie *Blow-Up*. Because I know that beneath this calm there lies the violence and love of blood, the love of power. I wonder if, as Hemingway said, the only way to know death is to drink fresh blood, in the early morning, from the slaughterhouse. For here everything blends, is endless. When am I free? And *then* what do I do?. How long can I remain so confused, out there in the fresh air? I'll have to see what's to become of me. I wonder. . . . And so the days slipped into wondering weeks and I found myself inside another bubble of heat and languor. My lawyer had put in a petition demanding my liberty. The judge had one month to decide my fate. The lawyer felt the overwhelming evidence in my behalf would surely elicit a reply of yes, freedom, from the judge. The whole procedure was lengthy, technical, and innovative for the small-town court. During the first week after the petition was submitted, after my parents and the lawyer had left, I arranged a special hearing with the judge. I felt that the judge had spoken with my parents and my lawyers; now it was time for him to really talk to me.

It was becoming increasingly difficult for me to exist, I thought, as I dressed for my afternoon appointment with the judge. I was going through major changes in my life, finding out that the days of letting my hair dry in the sky when I'm high were over. I was in prison, and despite all the little privileges I was given, such as walks in the courtyard and nice police guards, I was still in the slammer with no freedom, no privacy, and no contact with the sun, moon, or stars. But my biggest dilemma resulted from my head—not my physical surroundings. I wanted to go into the judge's chambers and tell him, "Hey, man, I cop to it. Dig me, I'm honest—I know the whole trip—don't give me any lip—I knew, I slew my tears with dope, which never leads to hope, but now Señor, I am changed, I know right from wrong, I sing a pure morning song, I wake up and know that drugs are what they are—drugs, *nada más,* and selling drugs is bad because people get hurt and I'm not selfish like 'that and to get money for something I didn't even work for is karmically B-A-D. So I've changed, let me go. . . . ." I thought of this as I followed the *Federales* out the door under the watchful eyes of the people and into the van, and out of the hospital, into the judge's office—and confronted with his little eyes and wrinkled shirt I knew that I could never, ever, under any circumstances, tell him the truth. He is so judicially oriented and no one really cares if I've changed or not in my heart—no one cares, only me and God. The judge just wants to try me with all the facts and do justice and put away the guilty. It is so strange, he holds my life in his hands and he knows very well what he is going to do. He talked to me about Jerusalem and the feelings of ancient cities and we talked of poetry, his favorite American poet is Walt Whitman. We talked of astrology, he is a Cancer, born July 23, and he believes in it. He told me that he hopes that I am not guilty because he will know it and use all the facts against me. I assured him that I was totally innocent, I was only living with Andrew; I didn't know what he did with his money or how he got it. The judge nodded and told me how much more he believed me since he met my parents, and what good people they were, and I lied more and told him I was innocent as the driven snow (driven over three continents and blown up my nose). I told him that I needed my freedom and he nodded in time to the fan which spun around oh-so-slowly in the heat and he told me he would consider all the facts and he hoped all would work out.

I left his office and followed the *Federales* back to the van, I wanted so much to go to the beach, but I couldn't. I knew the guards wouldn't go and I found myself back at the hospital in the terrible heat with Francisco solicitously smiling and motioning to me to get into my hospital gown quickly, which I did. When I returned from the bathroom after changing, Francisco was beaming and I looked out into the hallway and saw ten children, one wife, lots of tortillas, and years of strife written in the air. Francisco's little nut-colored children walked up one by one and shook my hands—all smelled of earth and Clorox, wide-eyed and fantasy-filled with dark little hands and clean nails. There were the twins in little Mickey Mouse dresses and the little boy, a fighter, a future *policía* with a black eye, and so on, and finally a thick, chocolate woman with a black braid and tender smiles who made me sit down and gave me a plate of tortillas with meat and vegetables that were aromatic and tasted divine. Francisco turned on the radio, the music came on and all the children started to dance, quietly, quietly, so no one would call attention to my cell, after all Francisco could be arrested for this little party. We ate and danced and played and sang and ate. Francisco marched around supervising, proud as a peacock, I wanted so much to give something to these folk who had given so much to me. I slipped into my cell and pulled out various odds and ends: a barrette of tortoise shell for one daughter, a shirt for the son, a ring for another, perfume for the eldest girl who was just coming to her womanhood, and finally, for the earth-mother wife, I gave my Chino original dress, knowing that she could never afford one like it, and feeling close enough to give it without worrying about embarrassment. I felt so close to these good people, these kind people who gathered their baskets and radios and clean linen and children sleepily to their breasts. They told me, the mother and all the little ones, that nightly they prayed for me because they knew I was honest and true and I kissed all the children good-by in the dark as they held hands to leave and Francisco, father, provider, lover, gave each of them a centavo for luck. And I lay on the bed, full of good food and friendliness and I felt guilty to the core of my soul for who I was and who they thought I was. I had so much to consider these days that turned to weeks so quickly, these hours, that I wanted to be true and couldn't because I had to lie to survive. Every morning I would wake up choking on a dream, a specter seen, and I would study my Spanish in solitude with only larks to sing descant to my chantings.

As I became more a part of the daily life at the hospital, the *comandante* more and more started to trust me. Lately, he had arranged for a widow of notable social standing to visit my cell three times a week and tutor me in Spanish. Rosa, my teacher, was very enamored of not only America, but of social standing. Tall and buxom, perpetually dressed in matronly dresses and nylons, she was a perfect snob. Rosa would step so ladylike and delicately into the cell with remorse for my intellect, which she felt was waning. She detested my street Spanish, with no conjugations, which all the poor people understood. She too would tell me not to listen so much to the guards, they are low class, this delicate lady would tell me, and I would laugh darkly as she gave me books of García Lorca's poetry about the earth and blood of the people. Everybody, my parents, my lawyers, my doctors and Spanish teachers would talk very elegantly in their sweat about the right kind of people to talk to and yet I wondered how they could judge who was right for me when I was in jail, a guilty dope smuggler, and the peasants were the only ones who really cared how I felt.

These false values became more and more apparent to me as August came in with wilted lettuce and melted ice cream. It was almost time for the judge to deliver his decision as to whether I could go home free with my father. I found myself praying nightly for an answer—getting progressively more and more nervous about release from jail and whether or not I could handle the outside world. I had been in jail almost three months with only my guard to talk to me of earth and stars. Nightly they would walk around with me in the hospital courtyard. There in the coolness of deep night under heavy trees with falling leaves we would debate man's fate. I would wonder if my changes hadn't come too late. Sometimes Francisco or Alberto would smuggle in beers and we would watch late-night alcoholics fall by the fence, or we would hear a dog chase the roosters around the yards or occasionally the lonely calls of two cats mating. And all the time my friends the police would assure me, soon Susana, soon you will be out, and still I wondered. I sat up wondering until the wee hours of the morning, please someone, tell me whether it matters at all if we live or not, I just don't care at all. It has lost all meaning. Here I am thinking in terms of going home to a house I never felt was mine, and never felt comfortable in. Why did I stop loving Andrew, and now no longer understand where he is coming from? I want to run away again, the pain in my head is unbearable. What do I lose at this point if I die? I know maybe now, at this point, there are no absolutes, I hope that this pain will go away, otherwise I can't live anymore. I feel so alone, no one understands. I want to escape from all this confusion and loneliness. I guess that I was incoherent, unable to relate to any identity. Do you know how long it took me to become coherent again? Neither do I. So I spent my nights, alone with despair, which managed to be everywhere, all the time. . . .

August 5, and I woke up and knew that a profound change had taken place, not only with me, but with nature. There had always been many butterflies in La Paz, and as I spent more time in the solitude and heat, I learned how to stalk the butterflies, catch them in my hands and release them through the slats in the windows. This day when I awoke I noticed that the air outside the hall windows was thick with butterflies. There were virtually millions of them in the sky, golden, orange, green, blue, maroon. It was like a butterfly convention with representatives from every butterfly color of the spectrum. I asked Salvatore what the occasion was and he told me that once a year, for reasons unknown to him, millions of butterflies converge in La Paz, maybe to mate or to wait for a sign from Jesus as to where to go to rest their souls. It was a beautiful convention. I knew that I needed someone to tell me where to go to rest my soul.

My father had arrived several days earlier. He had spent all of his time with me, in case I was losing my mind, which I wasn't. I was becoming clear for the first time in my life. My father and I talked very little; he was uncomfortable with me and worried about his own integrity, if it was being compromised in the whole situation. I couldn't look him in the eye. We played cards incessantly with my guards who sensed the tension and played to take everyone's mind off the problems. One day my father had revealed to me what he really thought of me when he had called me "a whorer of life." He felt that my self-destructiveness and decadent ways had pulled him and my mother into an impossible situation. This, I knew, was true; but his position was too paradoxical to be resolved. If he maintained his position that he would never pay anyone off or lie, then I might simply rot in jail. If it were known to the judge and district prosecutor that I had been busted before for smuggling hash into L.A., then I had no hope. So I knew that along with myself I placed my parents in jeopardy. They were unable to make moral or philosophical choices. I loved that man so and finally saw him humanly, for the first time in my life. My lawyer had also flown in from Mexico City to be present at the judge's decision. The bizarre quality of the whole situation was that my father had arrived to take me "home" and you can't go home again. The home in which I had grown up was left behind when I slowly rejected all those so-called middle-class values (oh, what a revolutionary!) and vagabonded my life away. If I were released, my father was there to take me home, where I could never tell the truth about who I was or what I had done. No one wanted to hear that.

My father arrived at about eleven o'clock looking calm and spiffy in his sports coat and he kissed me hello like, "Hello, Susan," very formally, and he took off his coat. "How are you feeling?" I wanted to shout, very confused, man, I'm very confused, but I knew that my father would tell me that I had good reason to be confused, his reason, of course; like why I had let myself become so decadent, and why my values were so far apart from his. However, my confusion went a lot further than that. We didn't have long to talk because

Francisco, lately overjoyed to see my father every day, asked him, via me and my Spanish, if he could help the hospital gardener fix the sprinkler. And the old, thin, brown, wrinkled slow-stepping earth-lover, dressed in browns and grays, and my Brooks Brothers, pink-shirted, business-executive, nimble-mover father, they made such an incongruous picture as I looked through the window slats in the hall. Three butterflies came toward the slats and I prayed that they wouldn't mistakenly venture through the spaces into the oppresively hot hallway which provided no exit for them. But heat and solitude had slowed me down, and overwhelming fear and time had worn me out, so I calmly walked up and slowly, slowly approached them with cupped hands, my hands made a kind of net, and they didn't shake, so I released those butterflies with peace and serenity through the window slats. They flew over again toward the gardener and my father who were both trying to overcome the language difficulty. They stood with hands pointed toward the sky indicating that it might rain, the skies might open up and release the precious water. That would make using the sprinkler unnecessary. Maybe, Señor, it would rain. I waited for my father to come dejectedly through the hospital doors and play a game of gin with Francisco and me. Francisco and I had played endless card games and he was excited to play with my father. My father sat down on the chair that little Francisco hustled to get him, and he wiped the sweat away from his eyes. Francisco's police uniform was beige, his skin brownish, my father's hand was chalky white, my hands started to shake again. *"Susanita, mucho calor, tu padre no está bien feliz."* I wanted to thank Francisco for telling me something I already knew. I know how unhappy my father is.

And I felt like shit at the sharp memory again (oh, why do memories have to remain so faithful?) of my gentle father two days earlier calling me that "whorer" of life and trying to speak softly to ask him if he thought that paying people off was any better, and he told me that he didn't pay anyone off. And then the hideous fear that he would stop helping me if I got too into discussing his values. Now we had to wait for the decision of the judge whether or not I was free, not guilty, the petition for liberty having been granted. Then, much like any other day the electricity went off, the small dumb fan stopped, time decided to take a break.

My lawyer, friend Joe walked in, jovial and red-faced. The card game stopped and Francisco nervously offered his chair to Joe, and my father, who rarely smokes, grabbed a cigarette and Joe shook his head and said, "Susan, the judge's answer is no—you can't have your freedom. But wait, before you hysterical" (his English was just like my Spanish), "all is good now, his next step, I give him four weeks to prove legally how are you guilty. And he cannot, poof, you go free. And he tell me, don't worry, she go free just look bad now if I let her go for public, so little time more. . . ." I felt better, fully understanding what Joe had said. The judge was worried about how he would look in the eyes of the public, he didn't want to look like he had been paid off. And with the legal process Joe had instituted, the judge now had to prove my guilt. That was going to be difficult, seeing as there *was* no tangible proof, only circumstantial evidence. So another month in jail was not so bad. I could wait, get things more straight. But suddenly, laughing after explaining to little Francisco what had happened in rapid Spanish, Joe sat back and said, "Only thing happen now is judge write to central office of Interpol to see if they have file on either Susan, Andrew or Ted. Check to see if any of them have arrests in other countries for drugs or whatever. . . . But no problem for you, Susan, your father tell me that you have no other trouble. So, four more weeks and I be back again. Don't worry you Susan, all is . . ."

I got up and went into the bathroom and threw up. Oh, my God, if the Mexican police investigated and found out that I had been busted in L.A., everything was over. All my lies about innocence wouldn't be believed, and the people that I had told them to, like the Judge, the D.A., the lawyer, they would feel like dupes, suckers. They would all know that I was guilty. All the days of worrying whether I deserved to get out of prison would be over, because I hadn't told the truth and now all would be found out, all my moral choices were made for me, determined by other actions I had taken. You can't live in a vacuum, everything you do catches up with you.

I felt like I was Steppenwolf, walking into hundreds of rooms, each one filled with more fantasy and more decadence and ugliness. All lies were the same, the same game where all went insane. I would now have to live with new fear, one that confirmed all of my old fears that to lie was worthless and hurt more than it ever could possibly help. It was like being busted all over again. Maybe in some ways the truth emerging would solve everything. Then no one could talk to me about values when no values were being revealed except everyone cover your own ass. Maybe if truth were revealed we could all take off our masks and deal from the same sky, laughingly, lovingly, and humanly. I was afraid of truth and I was afraid of lies.

Then I remembered an old Greek myth that when someone dies it is as if his soul emerges as a butterfly, his pure life essence emerges and flies high in the sky free of the body and physical problems. Maybe all these thousands of butterflies that were hovering over the hospitals were souls who had come to help me see that to really live is to be free in the physical as well as spiritual, and to not worry; I wondered if in my present position it was possible, so many decisions to be made. I knew that an old me had died forever, the one who thought that she could scheme, dream, and lie eternally, playing the big joke on everyone, thumbing her nose at the whole world of laws, and disciplines, and incidentally, peace of mind. I had only my truth now as I walked into the hallway in the middle of the butterfly convention. I picked a lavender butterfly to take my old self away and emerge the new Susan. She flew in through the slats out of all the thousands of butterflies that converged in the lush courtyard, right up to my waiting hands and rested delicately on them. She knew me, too. I gently encased her and thought of jails and busts and guilt and lies and knew that real bust, the real mind-killer took place in your head, where only you are in control. And I said goodby to my parents and lawyers and police and schools and friends and enemies and said hello to the earth and skies and trees and sea and I closed my eyes and sent my soul out that window with the butterfly. And I let myself be carried out on the wings of that gentle lady who was also me, going to a place where I can learn to greet my eyes with strength from inside me, where I will change and flow like the sea.

EDITOR'S NOTE

On September 22, 1972, Susan Nadler was released from prison. Her release was obtained through the efforts of counsel and an appeal based on points of Mexican law and rules of evidence. There were no payoffs, no miracles, no great escape.

She was lucky.

Hundreds of Americans now languishing in prisons all over the world have not been so fortunate. The road home for them is long and hard. This book has been written, in part, to keep their memories alive and to remind people of the Draconian penalties handed out for drug offenses in many countries.

CHAPTER X

A LONG WAY FROM HOME

IT WAS FOUR AM in La Paz, Mexico. The sky was dark blue, blue like the Pacific Ocean fifty miles from shore, blue like the imported cashmere sweater from Beverly Hills that I would never wear again, blue like Andrew's eyes the last time we swam at the beach. A falling star drizzled past the bars on the windows of my hospital cell. It had not shot out of the night like a free-wheeling cosmic dancer, but had fallen dejectedly behind the row of houses where Andrew and I had lived. My heart was beating in my throat. I faintly heard his steps coming down the corridor, padding softly on the outside strip of linoleum, the strip that didn't squeak, the silent strip he tried to stay within on his nightly visits to my cell.

Somewhere outside, a lone radio played. I recognized the plaintive melodic voice of Armando Monsinaro, one of Mexico's famous composers whom I had come to love since being in prison. He was singing my favorite song, "Yesterday It Rained." Julio was standing outside my cell door now. My solitary confinement cell door that was made entirely of corrugated iron bars. It permitted every guard and policia to look directly at me no matter what I was doing. I could already smell his scent of lilac from several feet away, and I quickly made out the outline of his giant sombrero in the velvet blue of night air.

Tiny Francisco, my beloved guard and friend, my companion in card games, my teacher of comic book Spanish, the provider of homemade tortillas, was unlocking my cell. I heard him whisper, "Si, Julio, yo soy aqui por todo el tiempo."

And then my cell door opened and Julio entered my world, my world of panic and heat, of memories and fears of never leaving, fear of a twenty-seven-year sentence, and my final fear of being let out to return to a world where I no longer belonged.

My eyes adjusted to the muted light and I saw he was wearing one of his several pale purple shirts. He was so clean and smelled of lilac cologne and Clorox. Julio was tall, perhaps six-five and large framed. He was the sublieutenant of the Baja Mexico Federales, an arm of the police that rode horses and acted like the Texas Rangers. His moustache was thin and black. He was so handsome, so virile, and from such an entirely different culture that I momentarily quivered. What was I doing?

"Hello, Baby," he whispered to me in his sexy voice, using the only two words he knew in English. Then he threw his sombrero on the table beside my bed, slipped his thirty-eight under my pillow, and crushed me in his arms.

"Baby, Baby, Baby," he whispered again as Francisco mysteriously disappeared from sight, down the hallway to guard for any errant nurses or interns who might mistakenly slip down the hallway and catch me, Susan Nadler, the so-called dangerous prisoner, the gringita, the drug smuggler supreme, the supposed head of the gang, and Julio, the gun-packing Federale, the Mexican who had killed over thirteen prisoners, the man who had captured renegades high in the hills of Durango, a hero of the police, catch us, two unlikely lovers, in each other's arms, hear our sighs and cries, our moans of passion and laughter, our attempts to communicate when neither one of us spoke the other's language. It was not safe what we were doing, not safe as he unbuttoned my snow-white hospital gown, my bata, and ran his fingers slowly down my thin chest, kissing the individual ribs that stuck out, massaging my back and wide shoulders, running his thumb over my thighs, which were covered in goose bumps despite the fact that it was at least 94 degrees outside and inside my cell. It was not safe as I grabbed his thick, pomaded black hair and forced his lips onto mine, felt his tongue run over the outline of my teeth, kissed his eyes and his neck as he tried to unbutton his shirt and I unlatched his belt, the one with the notches in it, the one with the mark for every man he had killed. And as Julio stood naked in the early light of dawn in the isolation cell in the hospital where I was confined, and he climbed gracefully into my bed, de-vouring my lips, my long hair, the mole on the side of my face, we knew that we had to hurry, because the soft light of morning was just beginning to break over the mountains, and soon would envelope the town of La Paz.

Somewhere, not far away from the hospital, a rooster crowed. "Ac-a-pul-coo," they all seemed to say. "Ac-a-pul-cooo," the bird welcomed the new day out of force of habit.

I knew that I would never see Acapulco again, would never swim on the shores of Las Brisas Hotel, or eat a fine meal at Carlos and Charley's. And I wept for my lost past and my stoned-out dreams of freedom. Julio caught his breath when a tree branch fell on the roof of my cell, because he thought he heard someone approaching. But nothing could stop him from cojoining with me. I pulled him on top and spread my legs slowly, inhaling the danger and culture of Mexico. Julio tasted of life, life outside the prison. He tasted of horses and guns and laughter and the sea and freedom. And I tasted to him like America and womanhood and forbidden fruit and tears and the future he would never know.

We two moved together in the narrow bed, on top of the stiff hospital sheets in the glow of the morning light, holding onto each other for dear life, coming together from opposite planets, understanding everything and nothing of who the other is and was, what the other wanted and dreamed. The rooster outside heralded the morning and Julio's heartbeat quickened. He had to leave soon. Or get caught by Adolpho, the head of the Federales, and lose his life.

"Baby," he whispered into my soaking wet hair. "Baby." He kissed the back of my neck and I held him tightly to me, never wanting to let go but knowing that we had been doomed before we had begun.

"Acapulcooo," the neighborhood bird crowed, "Acapulcooo," he warbled, to the sky and the sea and the air and the misty rays of the tropical morning.

"Acapulco," I cried to myself after Julio had left me, and I smelled the pillow where his head had lain and our hearts and souls had met. "Acapulco," I sobbed at my realization that today, August 19, 1972, Julio was my only contact with the world around me, and the mighty Mexican policeman might be my last, my last lover, my last man, my last touch with freedom and passion. My last dance with life as I had known it. I lay back in the damp humid hospital sheets and allowed the past to invade me.

I guess my real scenario with stepping over the edge began the first time I ever smoked marijuana. It happened in Greenwich Village when I was sixteen. No one in Squirrel Hill, the wealthy Jewish section where I grew up, or anywhere else in Pittsburgh that I knew, had even heard of marijuana. It was 1963 and my mother had taken me up to New York City, to the Plaza Hotel, for my birthday present. It was a great gift that I didn't appreciate. Back then I wore my hair short, my face was scrubbed clean, and I had on the de rigueur short white gloves. My mother's best friend Bunny had moved to New York City several years ago, after her gorgeous husband had died of Hodgkin's disease. I was definitely not prepared when her son Larry answered the door of Bunny's large West Village apartment. I was dressed all in white, short white dress with blue smocking, white gloves, bone-colored heels from B. Altman. And Larry was dressed all in black: black turtleneck, black pants, vest, even black gloves. He was almost handsome in a soft way. He had long brown hair that framed his face and green eyes that looked at me like I was the most conservative girl he had ever seen. I felt very awkward.

Larry was obviously part of a lifestyle I didn't know about, not even from all the books I read. Dinner was difficult; Larry and I tried to pay attention while our mothers, best friends for years, talked about old times, new jobs. Bunny was now involved in television production in New York. Neither one of us ate the charcoal-broiled steak and salad. Right after dinner, Larry asked me if I wanted to go hang out in the Village with him and meet some of the members of his band. Larry was a full-fledged musician. I played the classical flute. My teacher was the first flutist of the Pittsburgh Symphony. Larry knew the "Zombies" and Peter Gallagher. He was cool. I wasn't. My mother was nervous about my going out with hip Larry into the Village, the late night den of jazz musicians and Billie Holiday. But she consented even if Larry was dressed all in black.

I'll never forget the way the air smelled in New York that spring. It smelled of excitement and unfamiliar stimulation. The Village was another world. There were restaurants and coffee shops at every corner. Lights flashed. People hung out. A man was reading poetry on a corner. Larry gently held my arm and guided us to a downstairs cafe, where the skinny Armenian bartender seemed to know him. Two other members of his band were there, also dressed entirely in black. Larry walked up to them and their dialogue began.

"Hey, Man, I wanna cop a skinny one so the chick here from P-burg can burn with me, you got?" Larry seemed to be talking a foreign language. I really felt out of it. The waitress had long blond hair and wore a peasant skirt. Her ankles were adorned with beads. She had a look like she knew something that I didn't. In one moment I decided that I wanted to be in with these people. I was already a mini rebel. The past year I had been suspended from my private girls' school for harassing the librarian.

My suspension had been the humiliation of my family. There were very few Jewish girls permitted into this school, most of the members of the board of trustees were gentile, wealthy, influential business associates of my father. My rebellion had been a little thing, but the headmistress blew it way out of proportion. And my name became synonymous with trouble. My parents considered my suspension a momentary aberration. But I was completely embarrassed when I returned to school after two weeks. Certain girls, the key ones, the cool ones, never talked to me again. I had had to learn to hang out with the intellectuals. Something I would later be thankful about.

Larry copped a j, and we took the key from George to his pad, which was a block away. I desperately wanted to act like I was not afraid to try to smoke marijuana, but my heart was pounding in my eyes. Larry was very nonchalant. He opened the door to George's apartment and proceeded to tell me it was a "crash pad." The place was a mess. I had never encountered this kind of atmosphere before. A curtain of beads hung between the bathroom and the combination living room and bedroom. Pictures of Indian gods covered the walls; the bedspread was a dirty piece of madras material. Filthy glasses with cigarettes floating in them and old pizza cartons littered the floor. The one lamp in the pad was covered by a long, embroidered black scarf; so even when Larry turned on the light, it was not too bright.

"Sit down," he told me in his soft, soft voice. I carefully looked around. It was a far cry from my parents' large house, with its priceless antiques, oriental rugs, sculptures, maids, and classical music. I tried to find a seat where my white dress wouldn't get dirty. Maybe that was why Larry wore black. He turned on a radio.

"You like Miles?" he asked me as he took the long thin white cigarette from his vest pocket.

"Sure," I answered. I didn't know who Miles was.

Larry lit up the joint and inhaled deeply. I could not get comfortable on the bed, which squeaked no matter where I sat. There was a pair of dirty men's underpants on the floor next to me.

"Now, take a toke and hold it in as long as you can," Larry instructed as he passed me the joint, a ritual that was to become an emblem for my entire generation.

I was not entirely a novice in deceit. I had tried the conventional forms of rebellion. I had smoked Camels with Carly, my best friend, while we hid in the bathroom and opened up the window to get rid of the smell. We coughed a lot from the unfiltered tobacco, but I was not prepared for the pungent, sickly sweet taste of reefer. I looked at Larry in the diffused lighting, he was looking at me, and I decided to ask no questions and be cool at any costs. I took another long drag of the joint, and focused all of my attention on it. What I really wanted to do was to ask if the smoke would hurt me, or how I would feel from it, or if I was going to get sick. But I was too afraid, too afraid to appear not with it, so I sacrificed my feelings of anxiety and decided whatever would happen would happen. At least I would not seem to be a fool. This was a pattern that was to dominate the next decade and a half of my life. Try anything, no questions asked,

rather than admit how frightened I felt. Never let anyone
know how you really feel.

Larry took the joint back from me and turned the music
up. He lit one of the giant, perfumed candles that sat beside
the bed.

"You like incense?" he asked as he handed the joint back
to me.

"I guess," I answered, never having seen real incense before in my life. I filled my lungs with the smoke and listened
as the street noise of New York City became background to
Miles's music; horns honked like tubas, cars screeched like
violins, peoples' voices sounded like reed instruments. Reality was growing hazy.

I handed the joint back to Larry and watched his lips as he
deeply inhaled. By the time he handed it back to me I felt
very happy, laughing, light, young, but knowing in a way far
beyond my years. After I handed the joint back, the first
thing I did was take off my little white gloves and lean back
on the dirty bed. The apartment no longer felt strange. I
sensed that I had been here before. Everything seemed
deep. I felt an overwhelming hunger that I would later identify as "the munchies."

"Hey, I wish I had eaten that steak now," I told Larry who
looked like moving liquid.

"Well, we could order in a pizza," he gestured to the half
dozen Gino's boxes on the floor, "or," he rubbed his hands
through her hair, "we could stay here and . . ." Larry leaned
over to kiss me at the same time than I leaned forward to
touch his face in a way I had never touched a man before. I
might have been rebellious according to the upper-middle-
class values of Pittsburgh, but I had never allowed any boy
to go further than feeling me up. I really had no idea what
sex was all about, although I had read all the right books,
like *Summer Place*, and *Parrish*. It sounds naive today, but
what I was experiencing as Larry's lips engulfed mine in a
wet kiss was a drug-induced passion, a passion that was just

beginning to awaken. Passion that was timid, but overwhelming. In a few minutes, after we had finished the joint, I never wanted to leave Larry again, and when he unhooked my bra, I allowed him to touch my young breasts, knowing in my heart that perhaps I was going too far. But I didn't care. I laughed hysterically at everything with him. There were tears in my eyes as we talked about how we were both stifled in our homes, and how we both wanted to write poetry, and demonstrate for civil rights, and go to the Left Bank in Paris, learn about meditation and live forever. I did stop him when he tried to unbutton my dress. That was a little too much. But I felt closer to him in a shorter time than I had ever felt to any of my adolescent boyfriends.

The next morning when my mother tried to get me to go for my birthday haircut at the world-famous Kenneth's studio, I pretended that I had a headache. I told my disgruntled mother to go on by herself. I couldn't bear the wait for Larry. He sneaked up to my room at the Plaza and we smoked another reefer. We laughed and made out for hours until it was time to meet my mother for lunch at Schrafft's. I would not be so turned on by a man again for years and never quite with the same intensity. My little white gloves soon became a symbol of the past, dance classes, coming-out parties, Sunday School.

For the next two years marijuana was not accessible at all in Pittsburgh. Country clubbers and their children were not turned on. In the slightest. The biggest decision most of those women made was what dress to wear to the high holiday ceremonies at the Temple. Or how to redecorate their living rooms. Or where to go for the summers. It wasn't until 1966, when John, my closest friend, returned home from Columbia University for the summer that I even saw a joint again. Johnny spoke about nickel bags, and copping a buzz, being mellow, all the terms that the so-called hip crowd knew. After I smoked my next joint I became a regular toker for the next twenty or so years. I depended upon marijuana to alter my consciousness, to take me away from a reality that I later discovered was not so very bad. And always I tried to repeat the innocent and sensual high I had felt in Larry's arms, laughing my head off in Greenwich Village. A few times I thought I had it. But not really.

College was a very important issue at my house. Where would I go? Where would I live? What would I major in? I was finally accepted into the University of Wisconsin, in Madison. The decision was a family one. There were many arguments with my parents. My father was an extremely soft-spoken compassionate man, whose anger you could perceive only because his voice got softer. He was a very successful businessman. He didn't watch sports or drink with the boys. He liked to spend the weekend with us, his children, his three daughters, and Sundays he would take all the neighborhood gang to the museum to look at the dinosaur bones, and go to Isaly's for ice cream shakes. He and my mother seemed to have a perfect marriage. They never argued. He wore his pink Brooks Brothers shirts, and his Gucci loafers, and presided over our long mahogany dining room table, carefully carving the meat as the maid served the vegetables. My mother was a beautiful woman who had once sung opera and danced on the stage with Gene Kelly. She had given it all up to marry her college sweetheart, my father. Although World War II and family complications made it impossible for either one to finish their BA's, education was the issue in the house. How you scored, not how you felt. My mother had an art studio on the third floor of our home where she sculpted. She was quite good. She ran a perfect household, sometimes with three in help. The house was her showplace, the food was extraordinary, her clothes were the chicest, and her daughters the most cultured. Culture was also very important in my family. I had taken art, ballet, tap, eurythmics, and recorder and flute lessons all of my life and had fought constantly with my mother about practicing. My middle sister played the violin, and my youngest sister was a child prodigy on the piano.

All seemed perfect on the outside. A fairy-tale life with vacations to the Cape, family trips to the ballet and museums, books discussed, and ideas tossed about. But something was not right. I was rebellious from a young age. First of all I was a compulsive shoplifter, stealing little things, cheating on school exams, trying so hard to live up to my parents' expectations, which were nothing short of perfection.

After my suspension from private school, I appeared to get back on the track again, teaching Sunday School, winning the prestigious poetry prize in junior and senior year. But at night I had terrible insomnia and in the morning I never quite made it up for breakfast.

When I turned sixteen, I began to have horrible fights with my mother. These lasted into the wee hours of the morning. No one in the family was permitted to have anything wrong with him. If I liked Bob Dylan, they took that as a personal affront to their values; if I couldn't score well in math, it was because I wasn't trying hard enough, not because I didn't have the aptitude, which was really the case. I had very few opportunities to make my own decisions. Everything was decided for me. I wasn't asked how I felt, where I wanted to go, it was decided for me. I don't think I ever made a decision in my life until I was twenty-nine. I tried so hard to fit in with what my parents wanted that I had to lie to please them. I spun such phanta-magical scenarios of lies that sometimes even I didn't know what was the truth and what wasn't. And everything was based on how you looked on the outside.

By the time I was getting ready to go to college, it was decided that I would grow into a beauty. But I never cared much about clothes; I never wore makeup. I spent most of my time reading and writing poetry. I never even had my own style of dress until I was in my thirties. My mother sent me all my outfits, except my college uniform of turtle neck, boots, jeans, and peacoat.

The night before my big trip up to Madison, I sat in my third-floor room—my giant room I will remember all my life—and I looked out of one of the row of tiny windows. I could smell fall's arrival. Below me was the oak tree that David Glazer and I had carved our initials on. Next door Carly's mother, a world-famous concert pianist, was practicing the Brandenberg Concerto late into the night. I had just finished reading the *Alexandria Quartet* by Lawrence Durrell. I wanted to find that type of exotic existence for myself somewhere in the world. I knew that I was not meant to live the expected life, which was marrying a rich Jewish attorney and having children, settling into a routine of shopping and lunches and boredom. But what was I destined for? I had no idea, I never knew what I liked at this point, not even what I didn't like. I had no identity. I was scared to death to leave home, and yet I knew that if I didn't I would drown in my family. On my stereo, Joan Baez sang on about the "black haired boy." Suitcases of new clothes, still tagged, lay all over the brown wall-to-wall carpeting. And below, in their newly decorated bedroom, my parents were in their nightly positions.

Meanwhile, out in the world of the mid-1960s, events were conspiring to sweep me away into a storm I had no idea existed. Events that would seem to change the world, give people freedom, bring sanity back after the assassination of the beloved president John F. Kennedy. Give blacks equality. End the war in Vietnam. Give peace a chance. I was a tiny cog in this wheel of fortune. I would be an activist and a participant. And a flower child who never quite fit in. A searcher for identity. For attention. From my family who never knew who I was or what I wanted.

But I would find out.

The University of Wisconsin in the 1960s was one of the hotbeds of political radicalism. Wealthy middle-class sophomores in expensive boots and down parkas from back East ran chapters of SNCC, Score, and SDS. I lived in a very cushy plush dormitory, in a suite with living room, maid service, and a millionaire's daughter from Chicago as a roommate; but my tendency was to gravitate toward the dope-smoking rebels who gathered daily in the student union and talked about the inequality of life in America.

Sororities and fraternity boys weren't for me, homecoming was boring, and LSD was happening. However, Uncle Tim Leary never explained that to turn on was easy, dropping out only required a little guts; but tuning in, that was the trick. When in rapid succession Martin Luther King, Jr., and Bobby Kennedy were assassinated, I felt the urge to leave America, to go far away from the nightmare of Vietnam and torn-apart families and arguments with my father about integrating the unions.

Like most wealthy postwar American Jews, my parents had assimilated to the point of joining a Reform Temple. The precepts of my religious education required minimal attendance and were based on intellectual principles. Judaism was an ethical value system where integrity was foremost, and emotional attachment to a historic and often inexplicably unjust God was secondary.

I wanted something stronger in my life. I decided to take the money my grandfather had left me, savings he had accrued from years of operating one of the first scrap metal yards in Pittsburgh, and go to Israel the summer of my junior year in college for an archaeological dig at Ashod, one of the five holy cities of the Old Testament. I felt totally out of touch with my college roommates' idea of how they wanted to live their lives. So when I left the country in June 1968, I never had any intention of returning. Somehow, I didn't specifically know how; but in some way I knew I would find the means to stay in Israel. I managed to get a full scholarship to the Hebrew University by late August, based on my records from Wisconsin; and I found that housing was not a problem. Israel encouraged *Alia* (emigration) for bright young Americans who might contribute something to the growing nation.

By November I had dug in the ruins, had a small affair with a soldier, realized that almost all Israeli men looked better in uniforms, swam in the Sea of Galilee, been to Masada, and come down with pneumonia. Then I met the hip, handsome, Israeli Joel, who spoke seven languages and was a photographer, cameraman, painter, artist, student, and soldier—and who became my husband. What did I know then? I had an orgasm the first time we made love, and he was gorgeous and funny and intelligent and listened to Bob Dylan. I never knew then you could live with someone and not marry them. Nor did I know that marriage between two cultures is almost impossible.

The marriage was doomed from the beginning. I had no idea what living with a man or taking care of another person was all about; and Joel, one of the machismo Israelis who live as if each minute was his last, could not believe that marriage meant giving up one thing that he wanted to do. We took gobs of LSD, and I found myself mysteriously discontented for reasons beyond my control. I was desperately looking for my spirit—which was nowhere to be found.

Living in a foreign country had great merits, however, despite the fact that we argued every day. We took tiuls, or excursions, every weekend. We saw where Samson met Delilah, where King David was buried, and we spent a lot of time at a strange small pyramid right outside of Jerusalem where Absalom was buried. We ran from bombs and sympathized with the young country of Israel. I watched as my husband became more and more sympathetic to the Palestinian guerrillas because we had many Arab friends in the Old City where we lived. But as I became closer and closer to God, I got further and further away from my husband, who was more interested in painting cemeteries and distorted figures groping in hell. We smoked a lot of hashish, moved to the Armenian section of the Old City, and bought opium from the laundryman called Jacob's father. The Old City smelled of camels and pita bread and spices and exotic herbs like myrrh and cumin and rugs and Bedouins and tension.

My little *Alexandria Quartet* species of existence became harder and more confining. I wanted to get closer to Judaism, Joel wanted to get further away from the religion that would never let him forget the Holocaust nor the fact that his neighbors were his enemies. We hung out with expatriot hippies who lived in the Old City, and every weekend we had parties on top of the roof of the Petra Hotel, where we roasted legs of lambs and I made hash brownies. We traveled to London, Paris, Dublin, and Cyprus, smuggling hashish in giant tubes of shampoo and shaving creams—unafraid of being caught. We had no fear of the law. We were going to live forever. We took too many drugs, we had acid confrontations and there were occasional slaps for me. My husband used to tell me to go away for a while and not bother him.

One night in the Old City, at a party, I met Ivan, a seventeen-year-old Californian who talked to me of freedom and health food and sunshine and music and making love not war and tenderness, all the inexperience of youth and mescaline mellowness of LA—which was vacuous and good-vibrationed out with Jesus freaks, Krishna freaks, drug freaks, health freaks, and fuck freaks, but mellow man, very very mellow. And my husband, who was always too busy being productive to talk to me, told me to go talk to Ivan and his mystical rabbi friend. And so I talked to Ivan and his friend Rabbi Saul, the twenty-three-year-old Cabbalist. And Ivan and I talked and talked until we saw it rain from the same cloud, and I got divorced, and Ivan and I went to live on a mountaintop high in Jerusalem. But instead of studying spiritualism, we read Marvel comic books and marveled at love and methedrine. I copped morphine in Bethlehem from an Arab pharmacist who traded the vials of pure drugs the Brit-

ish had left after Israel's independence for ten trips of Purple Haze. I watched Ivan inject me with drugs. Maybe I
hoped to find something, some grain of purity in my arm
and instead I retreated further and further from reality into a
psychedelic mist. Life is so simple when your parents support you.

I finally received my BA from the American College in
Jerusalem, managing to write my papers stoned out on either seconals or methedrine. But Ivan had to return to the
United States. There was a five-year age difference between
us. Ivan was worried about how he would support me in LA.
We wanted to continue our dream in California and all that
we knew how to do was smuggle hash. So I sold my car, a
Fiat my parents had given me as a wedding gift, and we
found an Israeli Interpol official to send out the hash that
we bought in Beersheba inside religious books from a
Jerusalem yeshiva, because the rabbi who ran that yeshiva
also wanted to smuggle. Everyone was doing it. It was the
fastest way to make cash. I remember driving up to Mount
Zion in a terrific desert storm, a khamseen, or sandstorm,
and seeing this Hasidic rabbi, with his peyos and fur hat
flying, yelling at us because of the sloppy way we were pack-
ing the kilos in the Gommorah, and the Mishna, the Jewish
books of law and commentary on the law. The rabbi was
afraid we were trying to screw him. He was standing in front
of King David's tomb, near to the room where Christ supposedly held the Last Supper; and here we were in the holi-
est of all cities in the world, overlooking Jerusalem, and the
rabbi was yelling at me and Ivan because he thought we
were cheating him, yet he was smuggling drugs. It was too
surrealistic.

By the time we arrived in LA, Ivan's mother, a mad, im-
passioned survivor of Auschwitz, also an Orthodox Jew, had
called in a rabbi from the Eastwood division of the Khabad
house to help her because she had found the first hash shipment, which we stupidly had sent through the mail in hard-

bound copies of *The Godfather* and *Huckleberry Finn*. The rabbi called in a California official, who appeared at Ivan's mother's small pink West LA house with several FBI men, and they met us there. I was dressed in a multicolored cape and long Bedouin dress, I had blond hair, and Ivan was wearing a Bedouin shirt and had hair down to his shoulders. Because the official from the state was Jewish, we were never formally arrested, just scared. Ivan's mother called my parents in Pittsburgh to come help. They were so shocked by my blond hair and gaunt appearance that they didn't recognize me when I came to meet them at LAX. They were also shocked by the facts that I had left my husband for a young hippy, and was totally involved with drugs. My father was always very law abiding and he didn't want to do anything to jeopardize his integrity, especially if pay-offs were involved. He did help me out. But my parents judged me and what I had done.

My parents finally left LA when they realized I wasn't going to jail. And I was left with a dingy apartment on Olympic Boulevard behind a Chinese restaurant, dark roots in my hair, Ivan, no money, and the reality of working. This was all too much for our flimsy relationship to bear. We broke up, penniless, without our mountaintop. Ivan died about ten years ago from a drug overdose.

Between 1970 and 1971 time was of very little importance to me. I worked a series of offbeat movie-related jobs, script girling, delivering sandwiches, jobs I acquired through friends. Then I finally hit cocaine, the rich kids' drug. I discovered rock stars in Rolls-Royces collecting unemployment, and all the beautiful people who worked so hard to be mellow. I moved up to Benedict Canyon Drive with a coke dealer and made the scene. Sometimes in my travel from bed to bed or from city to city I would stop and say, wait a minute, what the hell, how did I get from twenty-one on a dig in Ashod, ban the bomb, at least reading a book, to twenty-five, still a lot of jive, Quaalude madness? Sometimes I thought if only I had enough money, I would buy land and not have to work and get straight and find God, the quest of my generation. But I never thought in terms of why not now, because when you fool yourself enough into talking about spiritualism, you start to have delusions of grandeur. You know, a little knowledge about Egyptology, a few joints of Acapulco gold, a few male reinforcements and I just knew I was Cleopatra this lifetime. I was divine. And when the Messiah came, which is sooner than anyone thought, I would be the one to walk in a white robe beside him and he would shine his everlasting light on me.

So I made the rounds of hipdom and ultimately ended up on a beach in Acapulco, in 1972, getting an airmail telegram from my attorneys that my long-forgotten automobile accident of two years ago had finally paid off. Please fly back immediately and collect $15,000. Do not pass go.

I returned to LA, split the money with my attorneys and physicians, and felt I was left with options for the first time. As it turned out, that same night I went to a party in Hollywood and ran into an old friend, a blond-haired, definitely full-on-in-the-divine, upper Hollywood bro, Gemini, songwriter, ex-Laurel-Canyon redwood lover. And he says to me, he says, "Hey sister . . ." And in Los Angeles, as in practically no other city in the world, relationships start very casually. The slightest raise of an eyebrow or candid smile smacks of invitation, the slightest sign, such as a rainbow reflection in the toaster behind you, and you know that you two are meant to be. So Andrew and I, we received our cosmic OK to begin a life together. We moved to an apartment in Hollywood, surrounded with mandalas and tie-dyed sheets, fur coverlets, and $200-a-pair sunglasses and a circle of friends who always included some fringe movie stars, some has-beens, some Sufi mystics, some health food addicts, and of course, some drug dealers. In our case, it was us. And we made plans to invest my money in a drug deal that would originate from Morocco and move on to La Paz, Baja, and Los Angeles. I imagined more and more that I was the living representation of Mata Hari. Everything felt glamorous and exciting, Technicolor and cinematic. Sometimes late at night, lying on Andrew's huge bed, smoking a giant joint, looking up as Venus seemed to kiss the moon, I would think of my father and mother, worrying about me in Pittsburgh, listening to my nasal telephone conversations and asking me what drug I was taking. They had just recovered from getting me out of trouble in the Jerusalem-LA caper. But I assured myself, Jackson Brown playing plaintively in the background, my parents would never know about this deal, they would never be a part of the La Paz scenario, I would never, ever be caught again. I was far too careful, sniff, sniff, pass the joint, my life was on the upswing now; there would be no trouble in paradise. All I had to worry about was making sure that I had the cash ready for Andrew's partner Ted, so that he could buy the hashish in Morocco, and have it built into an armoire there, and shipped to La Paz, which was a duty-free port, and pick it up at the tiny airport, where everyone would be too sleepy and languorous to notice, and have it built into a boat, to speed up the coast to Los Angeles, sell it to the distributor, collect my $40,000 and be home free. What could be easier?

Finally, Andrew got the telegram to leave. His job was to wait in La Paz for the package. I spent two lonely weeks in LA. I did a lot of dieting, smoking, writing, reading, and laundry. Then the phone rang and it was Andrew, whom I barely remembered. He told me to get on a plane the next morning; there was a ticket waiting for me at the airport. I was to bring a little money, some dugee, and some coke.

I carefully planned my travel outfit. I wore a large silver-and-turquoise cross some of the Sufi brothers had made, carried a tan leather case from Georgio's, checked to see if all the dope was in my makeup case, took two Quaaludes and fell asleep as the Air Mexico plane left LA.

The last words I remember hearing before I fell out on the plane came from a wealthy California real estate dealer who was going to deplane in Puerta Vallerta. "Baby," he laughed, taking off his shades and adjusting his collar, "people who love rock 'n' roll will never grow old."

The minute I stepped off the plane in La Paz I felt a wave of tropical desert heat that was overwhelming. I started sweating between my breasts. I immediately spotted Andrew, in his straw hat. He looked a lot like Richard Chamberlain as he crushed me in a sweaty embrace.

"Hey, Honey, que pasa with my baby?"

The La Paz airport was very clean, unlike the other Mexican airports where I had landed. I was painfully aware that despite all the years I had spent in Mexico, I had never bothered to learn any Spanish. I had been too stoned and too preoccupied. We jumped into the Safari Jeep that Andrew's so-called company rented. As we drove off I reassured him that I had brought along the dope. We drove past beaches and restaurants, down immaculate, steaming streets and my eyes searched La Paz for a beggar with an outstretched hand, so common in other parts of Mexico, but there were none.

The beach road was spectacular, the sand white and clear, the Sea of Coromel, aqua and teeming with fish. I would spend many days at this playa with Andrew.

Because La Paz is a duty-free port, much of its money comes from importing low and making marginal profit on perfume, sweaters, Oaxaca straw bags, Taxco silver, and mainland embroidered shirts. Large packages, such as the one our hashish was coming in, arouse very little suspicion. The tourists who frequented La Paz were primarily WASPy boating types. There were many yachts moored there, and an entire subculture of inbred fishermen scooted from boat to boat in small-water crafts. The town had no university, so most of the young people either left for Guadalajara University with dreams or stayed home with the reality of becoming busboys at one of the four hotels, waiters at the restaurants, fishermen, or police. Life was very simple there. The natives were friendly to Americans, not out to hustle them. The older sections of town, with the roosters that crowed to the tune of Ac-a-pul-coo, and the mud houses of red and ochres and browns looked like "Desolation Road" from Dylan's song. The city proper was small, but slightly sophisticated. The one modern building was the Hospital Salvitorre, across the street from our apartment.

La Paz literally translated means peace. It was calm there. It had an aura of some of the old Western towns of Utah and Wyoming. The crime rate was very low; no American had ever been busted for drugs; the police were the highest paid of the civil servants; there were a few tourists; a few orchata, or rice water, stands; a central *commercial*, or supermarket; many fresh fruit and tortilla stands; and much serenity and peace. But not for long.

Our apartment was modern, had two bedrooms, bathroom, kitchen, and dining room and living room combined; it smelled clean and like the sea. The decorations were from Morocco and India, left over from another dope shipment. Mandalas covered the walls, a little plastic sculpture of Krishna and his pals playing various instruments sat on the dining room table, and the doorways held chimes and mobiles from Tangiers and maps of Mexico. It was really like a cleaned-up version of the crashpad where I first got high. Andrew and I were a wealthy couple in land development; we went out to eat frequently, swam, stayed on an occasional yacht, and kept to ourselves. I wondered how long we could keep up that image. Then we started to get loaded and didn't care. Andrew told me that all the dope came from Mazatlan, and was good, the farmacia had all the Mandrax (the French equivalent of Quaalude) that we could eat, and with my good looks, who knew what else we could score. We had an all-expense paid trip to the hotlands, a beautiful apartment, all the drugs we wanted, we dug each other, and I had an assured forty grand coming. What else could you want, but a little brains, common sense, foresight, and self-respect?

Life for us went immediately downhill once I began to score drugs on a regular basis from the farmacia. The next month was one of oblivion. We swam and nodded out all day at the hot beach, drank fish soup, went home, made love, woke up, got high, planned what restaurant to go to for the evening, ate, and loaded on our asses, headed out to a steamy discotheque, drank banana daiquiris, and sensuously danced with a group of young Bajans clapping around us as if we were heroes. We had a certain charisma that all conspirators had: we knew something that no one else did.

And in the heat of the anticipation of the deal, under the influence of drugs, which we were now injecting, in the warmth and somnambulism, the lassitude of the tropical paradise, we soon began to fall into a romantic daze. We got lazy and sloppy. We wore out our welcome at every drugstore, we nodded out at all the restaurants, sometimes we were so stoned that we yelled at each other and the waiters. We wrung out our bodies and minds on methedrine, thinking we were organized, staying up all night writing lousy songs that we imagined were going to make us famous. We drove around town defiantly as if we owned it. We didn't obey the traffic signals, and we began to forget why we were there in the first place.

Three weeks had gone by and still no word from Ted about the package. Finally, with much trouble trying to walk straight, we made a long-distance phone call from one of the fancier hotels to Aero Cargo, the small national airline that was supposed to be flying the package in from Mexico City. The administrator told Andrew, one muggy afternoon, that the package had been sent four weeks ago from Morocco. We should have received it by now. This fact should have alerted us—we should have become suspicious, but we were far too stoned and far too confident in our divine protection. This date, approximately May 15, or around the day George Wallace was shot, marked the beginning of our descent from Lower Level Boogie to Looney Tunes. We ignored a warning from a friendly neighbor who was getting us heroin that strange men had been around asking questions about us. We were so zonked out that when Ted arrived, in his three-piece suit, and looked at me, sick from shooting so many drugs, and Andrew, who was babbling about our music, Ted tried to get me to leave. If I had left, I never would have got into trouble. But I didn't want to miss out on anything. I wanted to be there for the action. Despite my premonition that all was not right. I was afraid to act uncool.

Two days later, slightly cleaned up, the three of us went to the airport to pick up the package. Ted immediately noticed that the bottom of the armoire had been opened and reclosed. All the Mexican workers at the airport were staring at us with intense curiosity. We should have realized that the gig was up. But we didn't—or couldn't, or weren't meant to. And that afternoon, the armoire safely in our living room, the lifters well tipped, we were on our way to the travel agency to pick up my ticket back home. I had decided by now to go back to the states to see a doctor. Suddenly, like in the movies, there was a big knock at the apartment door. All I could think about was hiding my tiny remainder of coke and heroin on top of the closet. When I opened the door downstairs, I saw a huge Mexican (who turned out to be Julio), with a moustache, a sombrero, and a machine gun pointed at me. I looked at Andrew and he looked at me and I looked at him and I said, "Do you believe this?"

Suddenly there were thirty Mexican police and thirty machine guns pointed at us. I was thrown against the car and frisked; and people were racing back up to the apartment, breaking open the door. Two of the hombres identified themselves as FBI men and casually said to me, "Congratulations, Girlie, you are part of the first drug bust ever in

Baja—and yer in fer the longest and hottest summer of your life." Andrew was handcuffed. There was nothing but commotion. I was coming on to my Mandrax and getting belligerent. But I managed to stash the joints from my purse under the mattress of the bed. I denied over and over again that I had any idea what was in the armoire (only the best hashish any of the Mexicans would ever see). An older man, a Mexican who spoke English, checked my arm for track marks. I thanked God that I was so tan he couldn't see any of the abscesses.

Another man identified himself in all the tumult, with half of the excited neighborhood children at our front door and Federales breaking open the armoire with hatchets, as the district prosecutor. He told me (and I wondered how he knew my name and then realized that they had been watching us for God knows how long), "Susan, do you know how serious this is?"

And the tall, skinny FBI man in the hat told me as I began to cry that we had to have someone's name in the States to call to get help for me, and I spat out, "I don't need any help!"

Clothes were thrown all over the apartment, music and books were on the floor, and the other FBI man kept repeating to me that in Mexico you are guilty until proven innocent.

Then Andrew and Ted and I were hustled into police cars where we all swore to keep our mouths shut. Ted tried to reassure me, "Don't worry, we'll be out of here overnight. The brothers in Los Angeles will take care of everything."

Then suddenly we were at the jail, the Edificia M. Sobarzo, an old hospital with thick walls and a lot of police hanging around. They took us out of the car at gunpoint, in the hot noonday sun, and Andrew was dragged away toward the men's side and I was led away to the women's cell, in my cutoffs and transparent halter top, with at least forty pairs of male eyes following me.

There were no provisions in Mexico for female prisoners—only for prostitutes. The women's cell was small.
The police pushed me into a hole about fifteen by six feet,
very dark, dank, and filthy. And all there was, once the huge
cell door slammed shut, was a cement slab as a bed, a broken-down table, lice, huge spiders, and where the bathroom
should have been, there emanated an unutterable stench.
There was no toilet, no sink, no shower, just a small dripping faucet. Sitting in the corner was a woman in a long
nondescript dress, pregnant, holding her knees. Her face
was Mongoloid, she couldn't speak, and was apparently severely retarded. She sat there, in this huddle, with a few
scroungy boxes around, which contained her clothes, and
some old bread.

I was completely panic stricken. This couldn't be happening. The deal had seemed perfect. I again realized that I
spoke no Spanish, and if this woman proved to be violent, I
had no way to communicate with her or even to call for help,
since the guards had disappeared.

I had to urinate very badly, but aside from there being no
toilet, and appalling sanitary conditions, there was no way I
could go in the presence of that woman.

The incongruous fact about Juanita, as I quickly discovered the woman's name to be, was that she had hung a
clothesline in the bathroom to hang up some clothes she
washed in the dirty water. She was determined, in her bizarre condition, to remain clean, even in her perilous situation, and despite the fact that the dampness never permitted
anything to dry. I walked out of the bathroom with Juanita's
eyes following me. Carefully, I sat down on the floor in front
of the cell door. From this vantage point, I could see the
large and beautiful flowering tree that grew in front of the
cell. As the months wore on, I would adopt this tree as my
own, because it was the only sign of free and growing life
around me.

Outside, the huge wall to my right bounded the men's

side and had a guard on top of it, and a policia wandered to and fro. I was petrified.

By half past five a group of thirty policia was marching back to my cell. Maybe it was the gang rape the FBI man had predicted. I literally peed in my pants—hot urine ran down my leg. I ran to the bathroom and threw up in the hole. But no one came to my cell; they were only practicing.

The sun was setting behind the tree, and I knew that the ocean was in that direction. Suddenly, from behind my cell and through the door I had spotted, I heard pounding on the wall and yelling. Louder and louder. I was still frightened, and the effects of the drugs I had taken that morning were wearing off. Who was back there? Maybe Andrew. I ran and started pathetically pounding on the huge metal door in the middle of my cell wall, screaming, "Andrew! Andrew!" The louder I pounded, the louder they pounded, until I was crying and screaming and working myself up into a frenzy; and then the outside cell opened and four policia walked in. I felt my knees start to quake, and the policia looked at me quizzically and they motioned me aside and I moved back. The largest policeman took a giant key from his chain and opened the metal door. I rushed past him to see if Andrew was there and was grabbed by a small policeman with a moustache, who looked kindly at me with his huge brown eyes as if to say, I'm sorry, Señorita.

I tried to question the police to find out who was behind the door; and the fat tender policeman pointed to his head and made the universal sign for crazy. "Los locos," he kept saying. "Los locos."

I later found out that La Paz had no facility for the mentally disturbed. They were kept behind the women's cell in a huge area, where they were restrained and where their families could occasionally come to visit. But I didn't find that out then. After the police left, I was alone with the pregnant retarded woman. Then darkness came.

I was starved and huddled on the floor, afraid of the lice

on the bed. When the sun set, it turned slightly chilly. It was still May, and the evenings were breezy; the stars outside my cell were thick. My legs were covered with goose bumps and I felt nauseous. Suddenly, I heard a radio come on very loud and a rapid Spanish voice droned on and on— the news—and then my own name, Susan Beth Nadler, followed by the names of Ted and Andrew. I realized that we were big news. I was to hear my name every night for the next month, until I began to think they were talking about someone else. A guard came to my cell door to bring me a plate of food that my ex-landlord had sent over. I could not eat at all.

I sat on the floor shaking and began to doze off, the heroin and Mandrax beginning to leave my system. I was just beginning to drift away into memories when the light in the bathroom went on. I heard singing. Juanita came floating through the cell, naked—her long stringy black hair floating behind her and her thin, black-nippled breasts swinging, her pregnancy huge and somehow comforting. She danced and sang as if she didn't see me, which she probably didn't. She hummed to herself as she gracefully choreographed her own special dance of joy and impending motherhood. She wove her way back into the bathroom, where she set the tired red bucket under the faucet and sang to the droplets of water that fell slowly into her hands. Apparently night was the only time water came out of the faucet. Juanita produced a small bit of soap from her hand and washed herself, always singing, until she was clean. She used her dress for a towel, and combed her hair with her fingers. Then she shyly walked up to me and offered me the soap, which I refused. The dancer shook her head, danced back, put on another faded dress, turned out the light, and huddled into her corner to fall asleep. She was to repeat this eerie and somehow religious dance every night for the next month until they took her away, half crazed with pain, to have her child. The dance

added some circle of continuity to my strange life in the
Mexican prison.

I was repeatedly questioned by the district prosecutor
over the next several days about what had really happened.
They would come to get me when I was asleep on the floor
or at midday. When I was led outside, I wanted to run away.
But I didn't. I couldn't; I was guarded by the armed policia.
I denied ever having any knowledge of a drug-smuggling
plan, or of drugs themselves. The two FBI men told me before they left to return to San Diego to report back to the
newly formed DEA, and that if I gave them all the information I had, I would be let go. But that admission itself would
have been tantamount to admitting guilt. And the cops and
robbers' game seemed absurd at this point. I refused to talk,
somehow believing that Andrew and Ted would get me out,
somehow believing that I was not meant to spend the next
twenty-seven years of my life in prison. Twenty-seven years
was the potential sentence I would receive for my crimes:
acquisition, transportation, possession, and importation of
250 kilograms of hashish. In two months' time, another 250
kilos of hashish, addressed to Andrew, arrived at the airport.
It strengthened the case against us.

I stuck to my story. Andrew was a legitimate businessman.
I had gone with him to see legitimate real estate dealers
about land development for his and Ted's company. No, I
had never even smoked a joint in my life. Yes, I had a degree, a BA from the American College in Jerusalem. No,
Jerusalem was not the capital of Morocco. And then I was
taken, filthy and ill, back to jail to wait for my food and the
note that Andrew would pay one of the guards to bring to
me.

I spent most of my first three weeks in prison dreading
the phone call I knew I would have to make to my parents. I
couldn't put them through this ordeal again. I knew by now
that when you are in prison in a foreign country, you are

totally at the mercy of your captors, their laws, their language, their judicial system (or lack of system), their impression of who you were, what you did.

I received the phone call from my distraught parents one Saturday. My father told me over the static line, "The FBI just told us you're in one helluva mess. We're going to try to help you."

And then my mother: "You are killing your father. You are a whore."

And with that little bit of guilt, enough to last a lifetime, the lines went dead.

For the rest of the time until my parents arrived, I met with a hip LA lawyer, Alan Laughlin, whom Ted's people had sent to help us. He engineered several daring escapes for Americans in Mexican prisons. He also tried to pay off my judge's clerk, so my father refused to use him.

I sat in my cell in the evenings and lit a candle from the supplies that Ted's LA attorney had brought for me. Joni Mitchell sang on my tape recorder.

At about nine o'clock, a rather handsome face appeared at my cell door. It was Julio, the sublieutenant of the Federales, one of the men who had busted me. He stood there looking at me and finally asked, "Tu tienes miedo?"

I did not understand. I immediately raced over to get my new Spanish-English dictionary. *Miedo* meant "fear." I looked at the handsome man in the pale pastel shirt, wearing a giant sombrero and a .38 pistol at his waist. He looked like a leftover extra from Wyatt Earp. He motioned me over to the cell door and gave me a flower, a gardenia, through the cell bars. It smelled intoxicating, heady, exotic, free. I began to cry, and Julio tried to explain to me in sign language to smile, be happy. I walked away from the door and sat down on the cement bed. He finally left.

The next day I was brought some of my own clothes and told to prepare for court. I felt very sick, strangely tranquil, as if I was floating in a bubble. I was marched to an office, where Andrew and Ted were standing with Laughlin and a small Mexican man they identified as Mr. Gonzales, our new Mexican attorney.

He told me not to worry, I would be out by the afternoon. My hair was pulled back from my face in a ponytail. I had lost over ten pounds in the time I had been incarcerated. My arms were so thin that the trackmarks from the weeks of shooting drugs were standing out clearly.

"You look yellow, Baby," Andrew said, trying to break the silence.

"After the trial, the judge has twenty-four hours before pronouncing sentence," Laughlin told me during the nerve-wracking ride to court.

The judge greeted us at the door; he was late in arriving and was just opening up the courtroom. He was about five-one, was wearing a filthy short-sleeved gray shirt, and there was egg lodged in his moustache. He was approximately seventy years old and moved so slowly that Ted thought he was senile. I wanted to throw up. My life rested in this man's hands. He sat down at his desk and read through all the notes Laughlin had prepared; it took him about fifteen minutes.

Laughlin was taking a lot of pictures with his Nikon: the courthouse, the ride over from the jail. It was obvious to me that he was planning a breakout. I had put Band-Aids on my nipples to keep them from showing because I had no bra with me. I felt sure that the judge could see the Band-Aids.

Finally, my time to talk came. I felt like I was adrift. I told the judge, as Mr. Gonzales interpreted, that I had never known that Andrew was involved with drugs, that we did not live that type of existence, that I was an educated and responsible woman from a fine family. Obviously my arrest was a mistake.

The judge thanked me. Court was dismissed.

I rode back to the jail alone in the police van. I fell asleep exhausted that night. At three in the morning, I was awakened. A huge guard turned on the naked light bulb in my cell and threw a young woman on the floor. She was small and dark and dressed in a short, sleazy red dress. She was also drunk and belligerent as hell.

She threw up on the floor, and then she saw me. She grabbed me and started to kick and pull my hair. The cell suddenly stank of liquor and vomit. I had been paying the cleaning man to use Lysol. She was my first introduction to Mexican prostitutes. I spent a hideous night on the floor. What was going to happen to me?

Then I became very ill with typhoid fever and hepatitis (and I've never really recuperated from those diseases). I was sick a long time and went untreated. A local doctor diagnosed the typhoid and when the commandant found out what I had, he sent me to the hospital detention cell. It was located in the deserted tuberculosis ward of the hospital. I was feverish and hallucinating. The judge determined that we had to stay in prison for one year before we were to be sentenced. The newspaper headlines were the most unbelievable part of it all. The local reporter covering the crime beat, whom I never met, decided that I was the head of a crime ring that somehow encompassed the Mafia. I was in fact the head of the Mafia.

After they moved me to the hospital, one late night, the infamous commandante of the Federales came to visit me. He was a huge hairy man, dressed immaculately in a pearl-gray silk outfit. He was also incredibly educated. I was reading *Steppenwolf* at the time, and the first sentence he ever spoke to me was about his great love for Herman Hesse. It was difficult to reconcile this image with the facts that I knew about the man. He tracked down criminals with a vengeance, he himself rode up into the hills to shoot them down, he ran the prison with little compassion for criminals. He was unmarried and was said to like mainly prostitutes. He came racing into my cell at about two AM. At this point I had guards twenty-four hours a day. Each one had an eight-hour shift. So I grew to know these men well. Francisco, the tiny fat wonderful policia was on duty that night. The commandante blew in with five of his closest guards, including Julio, and woke me up, which was not difficult considering that I barely slept. He began to question me. I was sweating profusely, and was very weak.

He said, "Susan, we have information that you are head of the gang, a Mafia woman." I didn't know what to say. I realized that he had been reading the paper. He continued. "Your passport says you were in Morocco." I tried to reason with him, he was an educated man. My passport said Jerusalem. He wouldn't believe me. He continued to question me for over two hours, with his men around him smiling and agreeing with his every word. It was sickening. Apparently my parents had just left. Before leaving they had met with the judge, and my father, through a business associate in Mexico, had found me a new attorney, the best criminal attorney in Mexico City. The judge thought that my parents were a plant sent down by the Mafia. It was all so hilarious, and hideous. I told him that they were my parents.

"How could such nice people be related to a big drug dealer like you?" he concluded. I didn't know what to say. "Tell me the whole plot, Susan, and you'll be let out soon."

I had nothing to say. I knew by now that I would have no life with Andrew. I had hardly seen him during the last month since I had been moved to the hospital. My parents were insisting that I separate my case from his. It was their plan that I act as if I couldn't stand him, to make the judge see how outraged I was by my involvement in the whole matter. And I had constantly to lie to my parents and tell them that I didn't ever know what was going on, I was innocent, to placate them, yes, I am really who you raised me to be.

The commandante finally got so incensed by my attitude that he left. The next morning there were two armed guards at my door. The newest rumor was that I was trying to es-

cape. For the next three weeks there were Federales, with
loaded machine guns, at my door day and night.

There was no way for me to discern the truth about who
was who or what was what. I received cryptic notes from
Andrew saying one thing, and then a telephone call from my
parents, who were back in Pittsburgh preparing to return
again, telling me something else about what was going on in
La Paz. I was totally confused. I became prepared to accept
insanity as an alternative to spending my life in prison.
That's how my whole affair with Julio began—it was a life-
line to reality. I knew I had no future with him, and I felt
guilty about being unfaithful to Andrew—guilty about that.
That's how unstable I was. But Julio came to visit me every
night, with little presents: books, flowers, ice cream. He
smelled wonderful, like a man. He looked at me with such
wonder in his eyes.

I spent the next four months in a Mexican prison, from
June until the end of September. This was the hottest time
of the year, dog-day afternoons by anyone's standards. I ate,
slept, cried, prayed, lied, and learned Spanish in an open
cell, with only a windowless bathroom for privacy. When I
took a shower, I never turned on the hot water. The water
heater was on the roof, and the sun-heated water was blis-
teringly hot. My father bought me an electric fan, but all it
did was move the hot air around. I lived in a constant state
of anxiety. Francisco, the little guard, taught me Spanish by
using comic books. One night I was listening to the radio,
and the announcer, who was giving a lesson to Americans in
simple Spanish, used the word *arbol*. I tried to look it up in
my dictionary, but I couldn't find it. Francisco became very
animated, and ran over to my cell door with a comic book,
pointing madly to a tree. *Arbol*, he squealed, his little sau-
sage fingers dancing, "*Arbol*, Susanna," he repeated. Until I
realized that *arbol* meant tree. And so I became proficient in
street Spanish. My new attorney, who claimed he looked
like the Mexican Marlon Brando, used to tell me that I could

speak with the best of the people on the street. And it was the people of the street I grew to love.

The guards who spent eight hours a day with me all had families and these families all became a part of my life. Francisco's wife brought me food, home-cooked tortillas, refried beans, cooked pork with avocado, flan. And his children all brought pictures to my cell. The interns in the hospital, some of them poor young men who had worked their way through college doing manual labor, taught me to appreciate Garcia Lorca, and spoke to me about the green wind. I wrote poems for the judge in my new Spanish and read the daily newspapers slowly. Time passed.

My father came and stayed at the hotel where Andrew and I used to eat. He was very confused by the language business and the Mexican penal system. He had to rely on his attorney completely. He continued to maintain that he did not want to compromise his values by having to pay anyone off. He didn't have to worry. I was probably the only American prisoner in Mexico who had no one to pay off. No one. My fate remained in the hands of the judge. So I passed the days playing Mexican gin with my father and the police, eating ice cream, trying to regain my health and waiting. My attorney had decided the tack to use. He would make it incumbent on the judge to prove that I indeed had knowledge of the crime. The burden of proof was up to the seventy-year-old man with the egg in his moustache. All was calm until I discovered that the judge and the clever district prosecutor had written to Interpol to see if I had a record. I knew that I had an international record from my Israeli caper. My father had never told the attorney about it because he would not have taken on my case had he known. When I found this out I went into the bathroom and threw up. Caught in another wave of lies.

By September an unusual, natural La Paz phenomenon began. Millions of butterflies came to molt by the La Paz ocean. Every day several of the lilac or bright green ones

would fly into my cell through the bars and aimlessly fly
from wall to wall looking for an escape. I learned to stalk
these silent creatures, and form a net with my hands, catch-
ing the butterflies within, and helping them fly free outside
again. I had once read an old Greek myth that when a man
dies it is as if his soul emerges as a butterfly, his pure life
essence bursts forth and flies high in the sky, free of the
body and physical problems. Maybe all the butterflies who
were hovering over the hospital were really souls who had
come to help me see that to truly live is to be free in the
physical as well as the spiritual, and not to worry. I knew
that if I ever got out, an old me had to die forever. The me
that thought I could scheme, dream, and lie eternally, playing the big joke on everyone, thumbing my nose at the
whole world of laws and discipline, and incidentally, peace of
mind.

Of course I did get out. The record from Interpol didn't
exist; even if it had, Mexico was too disorganized to get it
through the proper channels. The judge couldn't prove that
I was guilty. I was sprung loose. The first night out I stayed
at a hotel with my attorney. While shaving, I gouged my leg.
Suddenly I wanted desperately to run back to my cell. What
lay ahead for me in life? Prison seemed safer than Pittsburgh.

Julio came to visit my hotel room, dressed in civilian
clothes. Suddenly, he didn't look romantic at all. I couldn't
make love with him. It seemed foolish and frightening. I just
wanted to get out of the country. Ted was let go a day after
me, but Andrew remained in jail for over a year, until
Laughlin broke him out in a dramatic escape involving the
death of a policeman. One of my old guards. A friend lost
forever.

When I look back on it today, I could blame the whole
thing on my parents, or the political and moral climate of the
1960s; but it was me. I couldn't bear to be the same as everyone else, I wanted my parents to notice me so badly, I

wanted to do anything to get attention, and I was young, pretty, rich, educated. I believed that I was immortal. I didn't recognize death—or fear. I was raised in a breakthrough generation of dreamers. We made fantasy come true. I had no idea of who I was, or where I was going to go. Perhaps my parents didn't properly prepare me for the future. Perhaps they never understood the world that they had created, the world that I was to be a part of. I wanted action and excitement. I rejected everything successful and rich, because inside I felt like such a failure. But the experience set me free. I broke out of drug use and shady deals. I came to face myself. I was a good girl gone bad. But I went good again. The past is permanently over for me. I was one of the lucky ones.

THE CRIME—Acquisition, transportation, importation, and possession of 500 kilos of hashish
THE SENTENCE—A potential twenty-seven years
Actual time served—Four and a half months

Made in the USA